COUNTY DURHAM AND DARLINGTON
FIRE & RESCUE SERVICE

COUNTY DURHAM AND DARLINGTON
FIRE & RESCUE SERVICE

RON HENDERSON

TEMPUS

To my mother, Leda, for retaining her faith in me.

First published 2007

Tempus Publishing Limited
The Mill, Brimscombe Port,
Stroud, Gloucestershire, GL5 2QG
www.tempus-publishing.com

British Library Cataloguing in Publication Data.
A catalogue record for this book is available from the British Library.

ISBN 978 0 7524 4179 5

Typesetting and origination by Tempus Publishing Limited.
Printed in Great Britain.

CONTENTS

ACKNOWLEDGEMENTS

Grateful thanks are accorded to the following for their help in the production of this history: Craig Godwin, County of Durham and Darlington Fire & Rescue Service historian, for his help and support with the brigade's photographic archives; also, from the same organisation, the chief executive Susan Johnson OBE and Cassandra Tebb for their faith and support with the project; Dennis Bradley for his assistance and Brian Spinks, brigade photographer, who assisted with some of the more up-to-date photographs on behalf of the brigade. Others who gave freely of information, photographs and the sharing of mutual interests and to whom the author is ever grateful include Dennis Barker, Brett Clayton, Ian Moore for proofreading and Norman Tarling, all long-term friends and fellow historians, and James Pope for starting the whole thing off. Thanks are also extended to Ray Marshall, the library staff and the editor of *Newcastle Chronicle & Journal* for access to their photographic archives and permission to reproduce some of the photographs, Durham County Public Records Office, Newcastle City Libraries and Darlington Library.

INTRODUCTION

The County Durham and Darlington Fire & Rescue Service is responsible for affording fire protection to a population of just over half a million people, both residential and industrial, within its borders of Cleveland and North Yorkshire to the south, Cumbria to the west and Tyne & Wear and Northumberland to the north. It is one of the smallest counties in England but in common with all other counties the population is reliant on the expertise and professionalism of its fire service in times of emergency involving loss of life and property from the ravages of fire and in certain cases of accidents.

Prior to the formation of the present fire authority in Durham the county had undergone some reduction in area and population through local government reorganisation acts that saw the south-eastern districts and northern districts transferred into the newly formed county boroughs of Hartlepool and Teesside and the new county of Tyne & Wear, but with some compensation afforded by the incorporation of the Borough of Darlington Fire Brigade.

This book sets out to describe the post-war history of the fire brigade in the county of Durham, beginning with its inception in 1948 to the present time. Whilst the professionalism and increasing technological skills of the nation's firefighters has never been in doubt, attaining the standards that prevail today has not come easily. The history describes the rudimentary equipment and premises that were inherited upon the formation of the brigade in 1948 and the constraints prevailing after the war that thwarted or delayed the proposals to modernise the brigade. It further describes the various reviews that have occurred during the post-war years and the local government reorganisation acts that saw the size of the county of Durham and its fire brigade reduced from a formative twenty-eight fire stations to the present fifteen sites. During the period covered, the more notable incidents are described, as are the developments in fire appliance design and the increased technological advancements in the role of the fire service resulting in the county fire authority title being enhanced by the addition of the word 'Rescue', in reflection of the increasingly varied and diverse roles of the modern firefighter.

In a publication of this size it is unfortunately not possible to mention everyone that has made a contribution to the professionalism of the fire and rescue services in Durham County, nor is it possible to mention every significant event and development that has occurred since the service was first formed in 1948 but it is hoped that this history will bring back fond memories to those who have had the privilege to serve within such a capacity. If it also enlightens the reader that the current professionalism and expertise has only been achieved by ongoing sacrifices, changes, and modernisation proposals, then it will have achieved its objective of publicising and preserving one of the nation's most illustrious and noble professions – the British fire service.

CHAPTER 1

THE FIRST DECADE

The origins of the County Durham and Darlington Fire & Rescue Service date back to 1948 when a countywide fire authority was formed after Britain's nationalised fire services were returned to local authority control. Prior to the Second World War there were several professional fire brigades in the county, set up by urban and rural district councils but the persistent air raids on Britain and the lack of uniformity in the nation's fire services prompted the Government to nationalise the fire services, thus for the first time bringing them all under one central control – the Home Office. In 1948, following the disbanding of the National Fire Service, all of the former Durham Urban and Rural District Council fire brigades came under one authority – the county council – although the county boroughs of Darlington, South Shields, Sunderland, West Hartlepool and Gateshead (which became a joint fire authority with Newcastle upon Tyne) returned to their pre-war autonomous state. The situation that occurred in all the nation's counties was the formation of new countywide fire authorities equipped predominantly with a mixture of pre-war and wartime-built fire stations, housing pre-war and wartime-standard fire appliances. The county of Durham encompassed an administrative area of 623,260 acres divided into urban areas of 225sqm and a rural area of 748sqm, with a population of 920,801.

One of the first tasks of the new county council and its Fire Brigade Committee, under the leadership of its first chairman, Councillor G.E. Pritchard JP, was to appoint someone to run the fire brigade. From a pool of 1,130 surplus National Fire Service officers there was ample choice and six potential candidates with the NFS rank of assistant fire force commander, fire force commander or chief regional fire officer were shortlisted and invited to attend an interview in London on 3 September 1947. Clifford Victor Hall from No.1 Fire Area Headquarters in Newcastle upon Tyne was duly appointed to the post. A former cadet-officer with the famous Cunard Line from 1920–26, Mr Hall commenced his fire service career in 1926 with Birmingham City Fire Brigade and, after moving to Willesden Borough Fire Brigade in 1934, he secured the position of chief officer of Beddington and Wallington Fire Brigade and Ambulance Service in 1940. Various promotions throughout the seven-year reign of the National Fire Service saw him attain the rank of fire force commander, deputy to the chief regional fire officer of the Newcastle upon Tyne area. In his curriculum vitae he expressed preference for a posting in a county brigade, particularly Surrey, Durham or Staffordshire.

Having appointed a chief fire officer it was then necessary to appoint other senior officers to assist with the day-to-day running of the brigade. Nineteen candidates were shortlisted for the positions of second and third officers and Charles Tozer, deputy sub area commander from the Holloway District of London, was appointed to the post of assistant chief fire officer. Coming from Britain's most famous fire service family, Tozer's career started with West Bromwich Fire and Ambulance Service in 1918 and within four years he had become chief officer of Blackpole Fire

Brigade in Worcestershire. Further moves saw him secure a position as the chief fire officer of the London and Thameshaven Oil Works Co. Fire Brigade in 1928 at the age of twenty-five, moving to Finchley in 1930. During the war he served as a column officer in the London Region. His CV described his considerable administrative and operational fire experience in high risk industrial areas including the City of London and the East End of London, including the dock areas, and also his experiences at the London Officers Training School where he gained considerable experience in organising the training of officers and men in the London region during his posting as director of studies and deputy to the fire force commander. The divisional officers initially appointed during the same recruiting process were J. Willis from Durham City who was to command the Stockton Division, E.C. Waters from West Hartlepool for the Hebburn Division and J.H.W. Brown from Sunderland to command the Durham Division. The latter candidate was also successful in attaining a position of chief fire officer at Wigan, which he accepted in preference to the Durham position, the vacancy then being filled by Mr J.W. Smith from Chester-le-Street.

One of the first duties of the new chief fire officer was the acceptance of an invitation from the Secretary of State to attend an inspection and display in London on 1 April 1948 to commemorate the transfer of the nation's nationalised fire services to the new fire authorities. The chief fire officer, chairman of the Fire Brigade Committee, deputy clerk of the county council and one nominated guest, Leading Fireman K.A. Johnson, duly attended. Durham's new chief fire officer was initially faced with the unenviable task of consolidating all of the county's former NFS resources such as manpower, premises and appliances into one cohesive force, a task that also necessitated establishing headquarters, transport workshops and central communications office or control room. A mutual aid scheme was drawn up with neighbouring county borough fire brigades where assistance could be offered to and from brigades in the cases of large fires or other special circumstances. A total of twenty-six former NFS fire stations were inherited by the new brigade consisting of the pre-war purpose-designed or converted fire stations at Seaham, Stockton and Stanley; the remainder comprising of wartime requisitioned buildings or those built as temporary fire stations by the NFS during the war. In addition, the National Coal Board Fire and Rescue Brigade covered parts of the county from their stations at Crook and Houghton-le-Spring under an agency agreement. The stations were incorporated into three divisions with control rooms situated in each of the divisional headquarters at Durham, Hebburn and Stockton. The stations attached to 'A' Division were Durham, Spennymoor, Bishop Auckland, Barnard Castle, Middleton in Teesdale, Stanhope, Stanley, Langley Park, Chester-le-Street and Consett. In 'B' Division were Hebburn, Birtley, Chopwell, Dunston, Felling, West Boldon, Washington, Ryhope and Seaham. Stockton Fire Station and Divisional Headquarters of 'C' Division controlled stations at Horden, Wheatley Hill, Hartlepool, Billingham, Sedgefield and Ferryhill. In Hartlepool there were two separate fire authorities, the county borough of West Hartlepool, whose fire brigade operated from one fire station in the centre of the borough and the borough of Hartlepool, which was covered by a retained fire station of Durham County Fire Brigade. Eleven of the fire stations were manned twenty-four hours by either whole-time firemen or a mixture of whole-time and retained personnel. The rest were retained fire stations manned by part-time firemen who were employed in other occupations but responded to the fire station from work or home when required. With the Home Office not approving the erection of any new buildings, a new purpose-built headquarters was out of the question and instead the headquarters was established at Newker House, Chester-le-Street, principally on a temporary basis upon agreement with the director of education whose department owned the building. Four rooms in the building were given over for fire brigade use. The new authority needed a name for the organisation and after many deliberations, a title that was most convenient for all purposes and the shortest form of nomenclature, 'Durham County Fire Brigade', was chosen.

Clifford Victor Hall, a former employee of the famous Cunard Line of steamships, commanded Durham County Fire Brigade from its formation in 1948 until his retirement in 1963.

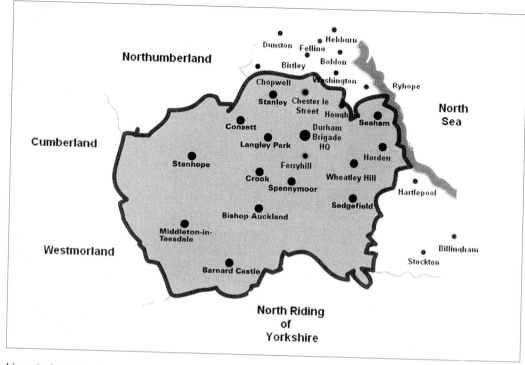

Upon its inception there were twenty-eight fire stations in the county of Durham. The shaded area corresponds roughly with the size of the county in 2000. The stations outside of the shaded area were all transferred to other authorities.

The official opening of the fire brigade headquarters took place on 22 May when a commemorative plaque was unveiled by Mr G.E. Pritchard, chairman of the Fire Brigade Committee. Two months before the official opening the premises had been in a dilapidated state and to make the accommodation habitable, within the limit of expenditure of the Home Office, the renovations were not put out to public contract but done by firemen who were described as having 'displayed commendable zeal and applied themselves to the duties diligently'. The plaque, made and inscribed by members of the brigade, commemorated not only the opening of the headquarters but also the work of the Fire Brigade Committee in organising the county fire brigade. After inspecting a guard of honour led by Divisional Officer Willis, the chairman inspected the premises (comprising staff and administrative offices, stores, kitchen and staff mess) and a parade of appliances. Incidental music was provided by the Easington Fire Service Band of ex-members of the fire service. Guests included the chief fire officer of Hong Kong Fire Brigade and the chief fire officers of Darlington, West Hartlepool, Middlesbrough, South Shields, Sunderland, Newcastle & Gateshead and Northumberland.

Non-firefighting personnel in the brigade numbered nineteen female and one male control room operators, fourteen civilian administration staff, eighteen cooks and two office cleaners. In addition there were four firemen/tradesmen at the brigade's workshops, later increased to ten. These were firemen/mechanics who, as well as maintaining the brigade's vehicles, also manned one of the appliances at Hebburn. The rest of the establishment was made up of 332 whole-time fire officers and firemen, some of whom were classed as temporary and 328 part-time or

The original brigade headquarters was located at Newker House, an Educational Authority building in West Lane, Chester-le-Street, until new premises were approved and built at Framwellgate Moor.

retained firemen for which there were ninety-seven vacancies still to be filled. The temporary firemen had enlisted in the NFS during the war and were due to be returned to the general workforce although some expressed a wish to remain in the fire service. In the absence of any determination of the total manpower establishment, approval of which had to be sought from the Home Office, the temporary firemen's contracts were renewed on a three-month basis. Of the fire engines inherited, many were in poor condition and required a constant amount of repair work to put them into a satisfactory condition. The number of fire engines totalled sixty, plus forty-six trailer pumps, nineteen ancillary vehicles and six motorcycles. This then was the strength of personnel and equipment transferred to the new county fire authority in 1948.

Following his appointment, the chief fire officer was required to submit to the Home Office proposals for the appliance and personnel allocation and manning, together with an appraisal of the current facilities. These proposals were either approved by the Home Office, disapproved, or returned for amendment. Part of the initial establishment specified two turntable ladder appliances of which the brigade only had one – a 60ft wartime hand-operated Austin-Merryweather vehicle at Stockton. On submitting a request to the Home Office the brigade received a second-hand pre-war Albion 85ft Merryweather that had been part of Exeter Fire Brigade's fleet before the war; this appliance was placed into service at Stockton and the hand-operated ladder went to Durham. To make things easier for the Durham firemen the 60ft hand-operated ladder was converted to power operation by the Home Office workshops at Wakefield.

The pride of Exeter before the war, the city's 1934 Albion-Merryweather 85ft turntable ladder was transferred to Durham in 1949 for use in the Stockton district.

Just six hours into the existence of the new brigade the first fire call was received, for Front Street, Dipton, to which one appliance from Stanley was despatched for a fire in an outbuilding used as a storeroom where the roof and floorboards were severely damaged. During the next eighteen hours the brigade was turned out to another two fires. Eighteen days passed before the first malicious false alarm was received: to a non-existent fire at Mulberry Terrace, New Kyo, also in Stanley's area. This precursor to a type of prank that increased in its frequency continued to plague the brigade for many years. In the first month a further ten malicious calls were dealt with together with 169 fires, thirteen chimney fires, ten false alarms with good intent and two special service calls. Most of the fires involved grass and trees being ignited owing to a spell of particularly dry weather.

As well as attending to fire calls there were many other factors to be addressed during the brigade's formative years, namely the recruitment of more firemen, especially part-time members, the replacing of obsolete and unsuitable premises and the replacement of obsolete fire appliances. The 106 firemen on temporary three-month contracts gained another three months extension and thereafter were employed on a month-to-month basis, although seventeen were quickly given permanent contracts. New regulations stipulating certain physical and educational qualifications precluded many of the temporary men from gaining permanent employment, prompting the Fire Brigades Union to put a good case forward that allowed those who did not meet all of the parameters but wanted to continue employment in the fire service to eventually gain a permanent position.

Of the county's twenty-six fire stations many were deemed as unsatisfactory for various reasons, with some in need of urgent replacement; the majority of premises consisting of prefabricated huts and garages, some with the addition of brick-built control rooms. The situation regarding the state of the individual fire stations at the formation of the brigade was as follows:

A1, Durham City, the Sands. A range of extremely dilapidated prefabricated huts with a brick-built control room and a five-bay garage built on land belonging to the Freemen of the City of Durham.

A2, Spennymoor, Silver Street. A brick-built control room and a four-bay garage of which two bays were allocated for use by the county ambulance service. These premises were in reasonably sound condition with no urgent need for adaptations.

A4, Bishop Auckland, North Bondgate. This station consisted of two prefabricated huts and a six-bay brick-built garage in poor condition. Badly sited and adversely affecting the operational efficiency whilst also hampering the recruitment of retained personnel. Urgent replacement was the only course of action.

A5, Barnard Castle, Crook Lane. Former commercial premises adapted for use during the reign of the NFS but suitable for some years to come.

A6, Middleton in Teesdale, Mastermans Place. Reasonably sited and although not entirely suitable was adequate for some years to come.

A7, Stanhope, Bridge Street. A reasonably well sited mixed prefabricated and brick structure in a fair state of repair although it lacked suitable drill and training facilities. A more permanent structure would be required at a later date.

A8, Langley Park, store buildings. A range of buildings used as stables, belonging to the Cooperative Society and completely unsatisfactory and unsanitary. Future developments here depended on the location of the new Durham City Fire Station.

A9, Consett. Park Avenue. Prefabricated huts and brick-built garage, in poor state of repair. Plans had been approved for the construction of a roadway cutting across the station yard making it necessary to consider the construction of a new station.

A10, Stanley, Front Street. A modern construction and in a good state of repair but the accommodation was inadequate. Additional dormitory space could be provided by extending the premises above the ground floor. Also the drill ground needed extending and a brick-built drill tower constructed.

A11, Chester-le-Street, Bullion Lane. Prefabricated and brick-built garages in a reasonable state of repair. The location in the Urban District Council works depot was obviously unsatisfactory and a preferable site was suggested on the northern end of Chester-le-Street, where cover could also be provided for Birtley.

A12, Birtley, Cottage Farm, Great North Road. This site comprised of an old house of two floors with a brick-built four-bay garage housing the appliance. All were in a reasonable state of repair.

B13, Chopwell, Chopwell Hotel. Urgent repairs were needed to the brick-built garage and watchroom.

B14, Dunston, Dunston Road. A prefabricated hut with brick-built garage and control room in a reasonable state of repair but badly sited. Consideration was given for the construction of a new station at or adjacent to the township of Blaydon on Tyne, at a later date.

B15, Felling, Carlisle Street. A brick-built building, formerly a private residence and a number of brick-built garages, plus a prefabricated hut erected in the grounds; all fairly satisfactory.

B16, Hebburn, Hedgeley Road. A large house and brick-built garages, one prefabricated hut used as transport stores and one corrugated iron garage used as transport workshops.

B17, West Boldon, Rectory Park. A new fire station was required at this location eventually, although the existing prefabricated and brick-built garage was sufficient for some time to come.

B18, Washington, Front Street. A brick-built garage and watchroom without recreational facilities. A standard fire engine could not be housed in the garage due to the low headroom, and the station was badly sited with extreme difficulties experienced in negotiating the narrow back lane but not sufficiently urgent to warrant inclusion in the current station replacement program.

B19, Ryhope, Black Road. A prefabricated hut and brick-built garage in a bad state of repair. The property was to close if and when the Home Office approved a revised establishment for Seaham. No further action other than urgent repairs.

B20, Seaham, Princess Road. Brick-built building, formerly part of a small isolation hospital with an unsatisfactory prefabricated hut – used for dormitory and messing purposes – as it took up space on the drill yard. It would be improved by the erection of another floor at the rear of the station.

C21, Horden, Sunderland Road. A commercial garage, leased from Eden Motor Co. and entirely unsuitable. To be closed when a new station opened in the proposed new town of Peterlee.

C22, Wheatley Hill, Wolmerhausen Street. Two condemned houses in immediate danger of collapse. A new station required as a matter of urgency.

C23, Hartlepool, Baltic Street. A brick-built garage with residential flat above, generally unsatisfactory. If the county of West Hartlepool built a new fire station nearer to the borough boundary the maintenance of a fire station would be unnecessary. On this basis it was sufficient for the time being.

C24, Billingham, Bellasis Lane. A badly sited brick-built garage and watchroom and prefabricated huts on the point of collapse and beyond repair. A new fire station was required in the northern sector. The premises were shared with the Urban District Council's works depot and the county ambulance service.

C25, Stockton, West Row. This station was in a reasonable state of repair but badly sited with the accommodation for appliances and drill facilities entirely unsatisfactory. A new station in Stockton but on a different site was desirable but not immediately urgent.

C26, Sedgefield, Ropers Garth. A brick-built watchroom and garage that did not conform to modern requirements but was sufficient for time to come.

C27, Ferryhill, Darlington Road. A brick and corrugated iron structure, formerly a commercial garage, partly sub-let to a haulage contractor but in a poor state of repair. It may prove unnecessary when the new station at Newton Aycliffe is built.

It can be seen that a massive post-war reconstruction programme was evident but many years were to pass before this could reach fruition. Government embargos on the release of steel and the necessary funding ensured that the replacement program would take over forty years before all of the fire stations were replaced by modern facilities. There were few purpose-built fire stations in the county of Durham before the war and although many of the district councils actually had fire brigades, most of the equipment was housed in garages or sheds, usually attached to the council works depots. The exceptions were Seaham, Stanley and Stockton, whose pre-war fire brigades were housed in purpose-built or adapted premises. Some of the fire stations were in an extremely dilapidated state and required urgent replacement whilst others, as far as suitability and replacement were concerned, were not such a priority. Already tentative plans had been made to address some of the problems inherited in 1948. The NFS fire station at Bedeburn Road, Jarrow, was closed on the inception of the county fire brigade in preference to premises at Hebburn that had been the region's Home Office zone stores. Although the drill tower here had been dismantled by the NFS, another one was erected by members of the brigade. At Langley Park, provisional proposals were to close the fire station and provide cover from a new Durham City Fire Station providing that a site became available in the northern extremes of the city. At Birtley, plans had already been approved to convert a kitchen and storeroom in the house into an appliance room, as there was some distance between the house and the appliance garage situated in the council yard. Although scheduled to undergo some conversion the station was also at risk of closure, as were those at West Boldon and Ryhope where alternative cover arrangements, to be agreed with the borough of Sunderland Fire Brigade, would see those stations surplus to requirements. The future of Hartlepool Fire Station on the headland was also discussed and it was surmised that when and if the neighbouring West Hartlepool County Council built a new fire station nearer to the borough boundary, fire cover might have been adequately provided by that organisation. Birtley Fire Station, however, was in a precarious position and was at risk from closure should a new station be built at Chester-le-Street that could cover both areas. In the south east of the county in 'C' Division, the remainder of the fire stations were deemed as being adequate for the time being, pending slight alterations to drill yards or the erection of drill towers, as was the situation at Stockton. The National Coal Board fire and rescue stations at Crook and Houghton-le-Spring were owned and maintained by the National Coal Board and did not come under the jurisdiction of the county council, other than being used on an agency basis to provide fire cover in selected parts of the county on financial terms agreed between the National Coal Board and the county council. The two stations in question were actually the most modern and suitable of all the Durham fire stations. Having been established in the early part of the century by the Durham and Northumberland Collieries Fire and Rescue Brigade to provide fire fighting and rescue facilities at all of the collieries within the counties of Durham and Northumberland, the organisation, funded by the colliery owners, was equipped with the most up-to-date appliances, with all personnel trained in the use of breathing apparatus. The stations were both modern, two-storey buildings with underground training galleries, drill grounds and houses for the brigade's men adjacent to the fire station. Prior to the Second World War the rescue brigade provided firefighting services to those individual urban and rural district councils that were prepared to pay an annual fee plus the operating costs whilst attending fires, and a similar arrangement continued with the post-war fire authority.

Regarding the fire engines, the new fire authority inherited a total of sixty fire appliances, of which thirty-four were pumping appliances comprising of self-propelled pumps, pump escapes and water tenders. These were almost all wartime standard fire appliances based on Austin, Bedford and Fordson chassis, supplemented by some pre-war former Urban District Council appliances mounted on Albion, Dennis and Leyland chassis; all but one of the pre-war vehicles being of open-topped Braidwood or New World style. In simple terms, the wartime appliances were mass-produced vehicles dating from 1939 onwards and based on standard lorry chassis with water tanks and separate driven pumps. The retained stations were equipped with Austin auxiliary towing vehicles (ATVs), another example of a wartime standard appliance, this type consisting of a box van-type vehicle carrying personnel and equipment and towing a trailer-mounted pump. Some of these vehicles were not able to be accommodated inside some of the fire station garages because of the low head room that existed and in these situations the appliances were converted to house the ladder inside the box body instead of on external roof gallows.

Durham City Fire Station at the Sands consisted of garages erected by the National Fire Service during the war. On the left are the garages where the fire appliances were housed. The remnants of the NFS insignia can still be seen on the wall.

Horden Fire Station, based in premises requisitioned from the Eden Motor Co. during the war, closed in 1954 when the new fire station at Peterlee opened. Note the scaffold framework for supporting the call-out siren.

Ferryhill Fire Station in March 1949. The sign to the extreme right of the building states, 'In case of fire operate switch for thirty seconds and wait to inform firemen of location of fire'. This action would have activated the call-out siren situated on the small wooden tower to the left of the garage.

In a similar manner to the fire stations, an appliance replacement program was urgently needed and provisions were made for an initial order of one dual-purpose appliance, two water tenders and two utility tenders. A further two additional new water tenders were allocated to the brigade by the Home Office. Whilst the proposals for modernising the brigade were ambitious, there were constant problems with the supplies of raw materials in the early post-war years and, in common with all other public utilities, every proposal and order had to be approved by the Secretary of State. There were long waiting lists and delays with the supply of appropriate new vehicle chassis, and the shortage of building steel and the priority of new housing schemes meant that the building of new stations was often deferred for many years. The initial delivery of new fire appliances was controlled by the Home Office that placed central contracts with appointed chassis and body builders, from which appliances would be allocated or offered to those brigades with the greatest needs. The delivery dates for new water tenders were currently in excess of two to three years, but for Durham the Home Office was prepared to grant priority delivery of two chassis and build them into water tenders to county council specifications. In December, two appliances – to be mounted onto Commer chassis – were ordered together with a Rolls-Royce-powered Dennis dual-purpose appliance with wheeled escape. The Commer chassis underwent modifications to fit them with special tyres and wheels, an extended power take-off so the equipment could be operated from the driver's cab, a fixed starting handle and bigger petrol tank. Two heavy-duty batteries, shock absorbers and servo-assisted brakes completed the modifications. A second-hand wheeled escape was also purchased from the Home Office. These were the first new appliances ordered by Durham County Fire Brigade. As a stopgap measure a number of wartime appliances underwent conversions by the Home Office, notably the ATVs which were fitted with small water tanks and hose reel equipment at a cost of £190 each.

Chester-le-Street Urban District Council bought this Albion-Merryweather Greenwich 'Salamander' motor pump in 1936. It was transferred to the county fire authority in 1948 and disposed of in 1954.

Washington's appliance was one of the first to undergo the conversion and was fitted with a 100-gallon water tank, in view of the poor water supplies in the district.

In the first year of the brigade's existence it was decided to establish a regional training school at Felling where recruits for the county fire service and those from other north-eastern fire brigades would undertake their basic eight weeks training as well as other areas of specialised training. According to the *Fire* magazine, the school was set up in a 'fine old-world house with spacious rooms which provide excellent facilities for dormitories, dining room, lecture room, watchroom and offices'. A large recreation room had been erected in the grounds and the extensive drill ground was surrounded by a neatly designed garden and lawn. As well as the large ten-roomed house with kitchen, there was also a three-bay fire station and a four-bay garage for housing the training school appliances as well as a steel scaffold drill tower. A particularly interesting feature at Felling was a breathing apparatus gallery, consisting of an outbuilding divided into three large sections, each communicating with the other by tunnels. Stairs, landings, obstacles and a maze formed part of the internal layout. Heat and dense smoke could be generated to various degrees to meet all requirements for trainees to qualify fully as breathing apparatus operators. Three appliances were required for use by the recruits and an approach to the Home Office for the supply of two additional pumps and one-pump escape saw the brigade receive one former NFS Fordson escape-carrying vehicle and two Albion Braidwood 700gpm major pumps that had formerly served with the London Fire Brigade. These appliances complemented another former London appliance, an escape-carrying tender fitted

These wartime converted mobile dam units formed the basis of many of the appliances inherited from the National Fire Service and were precursors of the modern water tender appliance.

with a 50ft wheeled escape and hose reel equipment based on a Dennis chassis, together with one Home Office towing vehicle and two trailer pumps. Also received free of charge from the Home Office at the same time were an additional auxiliary towing vehicle for use at Hartlepool and a wartime Fordson vehicle for conversion to an emergency tender. Station Officer Chapman from Stockton Fire Station was appointed as commandant of the training school on an initial eight-week probation. An interesting appliance housed at the training school was an old Bishop Auckland Shand Mason horse-drawn, steam fire engine that the council loaned to the brigade for exhibition in a proposed fire service museum on condition that it be kept in working order. Whilst the notion of a fire service museum in Durham was never pursued, the appliance still survives and is frequently seen at vintage vehicle events. It was later removed from Felling and handed over to Bowes Museum where it was felt it could be displayed to better effect. Displayed in the open air around the grounds were several old wooden manual fire engines; the exposure of which did little to prevent them from succumbing to the ravages of northern winters.

The first training course for new recruits commenced in June 1948 and was attended by nineteen firemen from North Riding of Yorkshire, Middlesbrough, Newcastle & Gateshead and Tynemouth fire brigades. On 6 September the chairman of the Fire Brigades' Committee and the vice chairman, Councillor J. Kell JP, officially opened the establishment and were treated to a drill display and fire prevention exhibition following the unveiling of an oak tablet, suitably inscribed by members of the brigade, in the main lecture room to commemorate the opening.

The first appliances ordered by the new county fire authority were a pair of Commer appliances, engineered in the Home Office workshops at Wakefield. This is the second of the pair and was ultra-modern in appearance when compared to the existing fleet. (J.C. Thompson collection)

The house at the Felling Fire Station complex, within which were the facilities for operational firemen and recruits at the training school. The training school relocated to Framwellgate Moor in 1963 and the fire station closed when the new Hebburn Fire Station opened.

The first fire engines at Felling Training School were a pair of former London Fire Brigade Albion motor pumps that had worked hard during the London Blitz and a Dennis escape carrier also from London. One of the Albions is pictured in 1949, working just as hard.

The adaptation, renovation, general preparation and subsequent maintenance of the school premises, appliances and exhibits were carried out entirely by brigade personnel. Henceforth the Home Office-approved training centre was in continual use with recruit courses and other courses, including weekend courses for the part-time firemen. For future recruits courses it was suggested that a fitting gesture would be for the best student to be awarded some tangible record of his achievements and it was decided that the most promising recruit of each course should be presented with a chromium-plated axe, the 'silver axe', suitably engraved. This tradition is still carried on today. The first Passing Out Parade for recruit firemen took place on 28 October and was followed immediately after by Recruits Course Two, with a total of fifteen candidates from Northumberland, Tynemouth, West Hartlepool, North Riding of Yorkshire, Middlesbrough and Darlington fire brigades. By mid-1949, eleven north-eastern brigades were using the training school.

Not long into the brigade's existence problems started to rear their ugly heads. First of all Washington Urban District Council submitted a letter expressing their concerns about the inadequacy of the fire service in that district and asked for the present brigade to be supplemented. One instance of concern occurred when, on being summoned to the fire station in response to the sounding of the call-out siren, no driver for the fire appliance turned up; all four drivers being employed on the same shift at the same colliery and not able to respond to the fire station.

In December 1948, High Usworth School at Washington was severely damaged in an early morning fire. High winds and a distinct water shortage aided the rapid spread of fire and it was not possible to obtain sufficient water for more than two jets from hydrants within a radius of 1 mile.

This 1892 Shand Mason steam fire engine, named *Nelson*, was donated to the brigade training school by Bishop Auckland Council and still survives to this day. Pictured with it are Station Officer Bill Tozer and Sub Officer E. Tindale.

Attempts to relay water from Washington 'F' Pit were thwarted when the colliery manager expressed concern that the drain on the water supply was likely to jeopardise the safety of the pit, so the pump was stopped. Apparently the brigade was not called until the building was well alight and by the arrival of the fire brigade the roof had already collapsed.

Problems occurred at Jarrow with its plethora of railway crossings in the district, all prone to delaying the progress of fire appliances as railway locomotives hauled their trains to and from the coal staithes on the river Tyne. At the request of the council enquiries were made regarding the placing of alarm bells on level crossings that could be controlled by the fire station at Hebburn, in order to give advance warning to the crossing keepers of fire appliances. In reality, it became doubtful that the railway authorities would grant priority to road users and so the idea was not pursued.

A demonstration at the training school of the rudimentary appliances in service at the inception of the brigade. This one is basically a drop-side lorry with a demountable pump and a water tank.

The fire station and training school garages at Felling. On the left are three former London Fire Brigade appliances belonging to the training school and on the right is the operational fire station housing two wartime standard appliances and a former Stockton-on-Tees Dennis Light four-motor pump.

'Passing out Parades' of recruit firemen at Felling were an elaborate affair attended by the regions chief fire officers. Ten such officers, including Messrs Mckenzie from Newcastle & Gateshead, Muir from Northumberland and Hall from Durham, watch intently as an end of course display is demonstrated.

Accidents involving fire appliances occasionally happened and just two months into the brigade's history Barnard Castle's ATV appliance turned over and was totally wrecked, spreading its personnel and equipment across the roadway, fortunately without serious injury to the crew. In November a pump escape from Hebburn was run into from the rear during thick fog by a Northern bus, causing severe damage to the wheeled escape. The procedure at the time with Home Office vehicles was for the repairs to be undertaken in Home Office workshop facilities, but the lengthy times taken to repair equipment prompted the brigade to undertake the repairs in the brigade's own workshops at Hebburn. Within four and a half working days the apparatus was repaired and placed back into service.

The sounding of air-raid sirens to alert the part-time firemen was the origin of complaints from several councils, notably those at Consett, Chester-le-Street, Birtley and Seaham. Having had to endure this warning sound throughout the war the public were naturally quite anxious not to be reminded of the lengthy wartime austerity measures that had been tolerated by the population of Britain. Apart from the use of maroons, an equally noisy alternative, the air-raid siren – as a convenient means of alerting the part-time firemen during the day and call bells in the homes at night – was the most appropriate method at the time and continued as such for the next two decades and more.

By the end of the first year of the new county fire authority's existence, a full survey had been undertaken of the new brigade, most of the manpower posts had been filled and proposals regarding improvements and modernisation to be carried out during the succeeding years had been formulated. The survey of the county's fire stations revealed that all were generally in an unsatisfactory condition,

Seaham Fire Station was the site of a number of complaints regarding the sounding of the call-out siren for summoning the part-time firemen to duty. Pictured in 1952, the siren is in the little black louvered box above the name board.

except Seaham and Stanley, and after careful consideration of all the relevant factors, a programme of building construction and adaptations to be carried out in the following five years determined that the priorities were new brigade headquarters, a training school, stores and a five-bay operational fire station at Durham City, new fire stations at Wheatley Hill, Bishop Auckland, Aycliffe, Billingham, and Consett; extensions and adaptations to the fire stations at Felling, Stanley and Seaham and the erection of sixteen houses for the brigade's senior officers. A total of 1,247 calls, including 140 chimney fires, had been dealt with. Ninety-eight of the calls were to false alarms, of which forty-one were malicious, and 102 calls were classed as special service calls (calls were there was no actual fire but brigade attendance was required). The busiest stations were Stockton, with a total of 159 calls, followed by Hebburn and Stanley. Of the retained fire stations Birtley was the busiest with thirty-six calls and Middleton in Teesdale the quietest with three. The ninety-nine temporary firemen had been whittled down to thirty-five. Thirty-eight had been absorbed into the brigade, eight had been taken on by the county ambulance service and the others resigned to taken up employment elsewhere. Many problems of the reorganised post-war county fire brigade had been complicated by difficulties of lack of manpower, supplies and restrictions and inadequate accommodation. These hindrances continued to plague the brigade for some years to come.

January 1949 was not a good month for serious fires with Washington council offices, the Fox and Hounds Hotel, Lumley, Stoneygate Farm, Houghton-le-Spring, Grange Villa Working Men's Club and Elite Buildings, Front Street, Stanley, all suffering major damage by fire. Newcastle & Gateshead Joint Fire Service assisted at the council offices, Washington, where eight pumps eventually attended, just over one month after the Washington crew battled the major school fire at High Usworth. The town's council offices in the old village suffered severe damage to the upper floors and roof to a cost of £10,000. At 3.55 a.m. on 7 January, just ninety minutes after the call for the Washington council offices, the Fox and Hounds Hotel at Lumley was reported to be on fire. Indeed it was and seven pumps attended this fire that caused damage to the extent of £11,000. Two days later Grange Villa Working Men's Club burned down. In March the Chemika Paint Works, Station Lane, Birtley, suffered a severe fire that resulted in the entire destruction of one of the plant's buildings. Two country mansions also succumbed to the ravages of fire in February 1949. The entire building and contents of High Croft at Whitburn, a fifteen-room, two-storey mansion, were destroyed and seven days later, Herds House at Croxdale was also severely damaged by fire.

On 27 April 1949 the brigade was faced with its biggest operational commitment to date when it was called in to assist West Hartlepool Fire Brigade at what remains the biggest peacetime fire ever to occur in the north-eastern region. At 8.37 p.m. West Hartlepool firefighters, under the command of Chief Fire Officer Kettlewell, were called out to a fire at Carr House timber storage grounds, Seaton Carew, where, on arrival, it was found that an area of timber with a frontage of about ten stacks and extending a considerable distance to the rear was well alight. The flames were over 100ft in height with flying embers, sparks and radiating heat making the approach very hazardous and rapidly increasing the fire area. The area involved was in the most inaccessible corner of the 65-acre site and it was necessary to approach by a rough country lane and thence cross fields to get the pump into position at a nearby stream. Three jets were quickly brought to bear on the fire but strong westerly winds and a dry winter and early spring that had dried out all the timber, sawdust and vegetation caused the fire to spread directly into the most thickly stacked area of the yard putting the entire site at risk. Reinforcing pumps from Durham were ordered onto the fire, which enabled extra hose lines to be laid out from the town's water mains some 2,000ft distant. By 9.15 p.m. five good jets were playing water onto the fire, three from the stream and two from the roadway, but then disaster struck. The jets from the stream started to crackle badly and furious explosions occurred as the water made contact with the blazing timber. All the firemen within range, including the chief fire officer, were covered with a hot bituminous product and badly burned about the face, eyes and hands. The pumps from the stream had to be shut down and it was later discovered that waste products from a nearby factory had contaminated this supply. The loss of this water was a severe blow at such a vital period and, before alternative supplies could be established, the fire had spread 100ft in each direction. By 2 a.m. the following day ten pumps were on the scene. A change of wind direction caused the blaze to spread in a westerly direction, prompting an appeal for police, civilian workers and volunteers to make breaks in the props some 150ft away whilst the fire brigade endeavoured to reduce the speed of spread by concentrating the maximum number of jets in this area, although radiating heat was causing stacks 50ft away to burst into flames. One and a half hours later the military were asked to send seventy soldiers to help move the timber and this number was gradually increased until 1,000 military personnel were on the scene. Despite the additional manpower sent to the scene the firebreaks could not be held and at 4.30 a.m. all firemen were withdrawn to the main firebreak. At 9 a.m. the fire raged on. The previous twelve hours had taken its toll on both men and machines with the majority of the first West Hartlepool crew having to seek medical attention and both appliances placed out of commission owing to contamination by the bitumous effluent from the stream. Shortly after, Chief Fire Officer Kettlewell collapsed and had to be detained in hospital. During the next hour every member of the West Hartlepool Fire Brigade was taken to hospital for treatment to eyes and burns received. In view of the fact that by this time there were more Durham County Fire Brigade appliances at the fire than any others, control of the fire was handed over to Chief Fire Officer Hall. By lunchtime the situation was such that the fire was still spreading and additional water was being drawn from the North Sea by pumps manhandled along the beach. Twelve jets were now in operation and the fire situation was determined as 'still precarious'. Another change of wind direction caused the fire to spread in a southerly direction, threatening residential properties and resulting in the evacuation of the householders and people working in the southern most section of the yard. The number of pumps on the scene was increased to forty and deluge sets ordered in together with searchlights from the Territorial Army and Royal Air Force. Two tractors were also borrowed to move pumps over the wet sands on the beach. As quickly as the reinforcing pumps arrived they were placed in position and, by 8 p.m., thirty-three lines of hose were in use. With all of these extra resources the fire was placed under control at 3.16 a.m. on 29 April. Chief Fire Officer Kettlewell returned to the fire ground at 7 a.m. and was joined in the afternoon by the Home Secretary Mr Chuter Ede. In all, some 25,000 standards of timber and thirty-eight railway wagons were destroyed in the fire but 40 acres of closely stacked timber in its path were saved. The provisional loss to property exceeded £500,000. Clearly the extent of this fire was well in excess of the appliances that could be handled by the borough fire brigade and, in total, ten fire brigades from as far north as Northumberland sent appliances to the fire, plus a voluntary crew from Salford, Lancashire, headed by that brigade's chief fire officer. The mobilisation required demonstrated the co-operation that was freely given during the early months of the new post-war fire brigades. Durham County Fire Brigade sent forty-five fire appliances and various items of special equipment manned by a total of 225 officers and men. All personnel of the brigades attending were commended by the Secretary of State, and in Durham personnel particularly worthy of commendation included George Strangeways, the brigade's transport officer. Although not a uniformed member, he assumed responsibility for securing water supplies from the sea and by the execution of initiative and ingenuity succeeded in obtaining and maintaining a constant supply from nineteen trailer pumps which had to be moved constantly as the tide ebbed and flowed. Despite no protective clothing or uniform, during the greater part of fifteen hours he worked waist deep in the sea until it was decided to order him from duty, as he was in a temporary distressed physical condition. Divisional Officer Smith was in attendance at the fire for twenty-two hours and Assistant Chief Fire Officer Tozer took over the responsibility for brigade control and the mobilising of reinforcing appliances, remaining on constant duty in the control room for almost fifty hours. Durham County Fire Brigade had had its baptism of fire, albeit in a neighbouring brigade's area, but it proved an expensive exercise. Seventy different items of equipment were lost including 102 lengths of hose, fifteen branch pipes, eleven spades and twelve teaspoons! After the insurance claims the fire still cost the county council £700. This was Hartlepool's second big timber yard fire. In 1922 a fire at Horsley's Timber Yard destroyed several streets of houses, making 100 people homeless, and caused damage – estimated at today's costs – of £36.5 million. The town clerk of West Hartlepool County Council expressed his sincere thanks to all the organisations and individuals for the very ready help and co-operation which was given so unstintingly and for the bravery, devotion to duty and self-effacing efforts that all who helped to combat the fire so conspicuously displayed. The manager of the Docks and Inland Waterways Executive was also most complimentary of the fire brigade's efforts and a letter submitted to the county council described how Chief Fire Officer Hall:

… stepped into the breach and there was no doubt that his outstanding leadership and masterly handling of the fire was primarily responsible for the successful containment of the fire. All of us have good reason to be grossly indebted to this officer and no words can adequately express our gratitude to him and his men.

Resulting from this fire and the complex mobilising procedures for the reinforcing of appliances, a meeting was convened between the chief fire officers of the north-east fire brigades to discuss the arrangements to be made in case of similar occurrences.

During the Seaton Carew fire it had become obvious that county borough brigades, when only one man was on duty in the control room, found it difficult to organise the necessary mobilisation of large numbers of appliances, so under the chairmanship of Chief Fire Officer Hall discussion took place regarding the drawing up of predetermined arrangements whereby the smaller brigade would be relieved of such responsibilities in abnormal circumstances. It was provisionally agreed that the county fire authorities of Durham, Northumberland and North Riding of Yorkshire would each assume responsibility for mobilising in a particular 'zone' as and when necessary. His Majesty's Inspector of Fire Services readily intimated that the Home Office would welcome such an arrangement as similar schemes were already in operation in other parts of the country. The scheme, devised to accommodate the brigades in No.2 District, i.e. Durham, South Shields, Sunderland, Darlington and West Hartlepool, became operative at midnight on 30 March 1951.

In May 1949 His Majesty's Inspector of Fire Services, Mr Percy Booth OBE, paid a visit to Durham County Fire Brigade, the first of many annual visits to test the performance of the brigade. Following an inspection of the headquarters' building, visits were made to brigade and divisional controls, the photographic section and workshops. A successful parade and march-past of 200 officers and men and twenty appliances was held at Durham City during the inspection. At the brigade training school Mr Booth gave a lecture on 'The History of the Fire Service' to the recruits. Ironically Booth was an early applicant for the post of chief fire officer of Durham and was placed on the supplementary list together with another twelve hopeful applicants. To mark the completion of the third recruits' training course at Felling, what became a traditional passing out parade and display, was held before a large gathering which included Councillor

Above: In order to overcome water shortages at Seaton Carew, trailer pumps were manhandled onto the beach where an unlimited supply of water was obtainable, although the pumps had to be constantly moved to cater for the ebb and flow of the tide.

Right: Brigade Transport Officer George Strangeways on occasions worked waist deep in the North Sea to keep the trailer pumps supplied with water during the Seaton Carew Timber Yard fire.

Opposite: The biggest fire to have occurred in the north-east of England was at Seaton Carew Timber Yard near West Hartlepool in April 1949. 225 officers and men from Durham County Fire Brigade together with personnel from other brigades and the military assisted West Hartlepool Fire Brigade at this blaze.

Pritchard, the deputy county clerk, and several chief fire officers from the north-east brigades. Thirty recruits participated in the display with the silver axe being awarded to Fireman J. Cathcart of West Hartlepool Fire Brigade.

During the same month another letter was received from Consett Urban District Council regarding the noises from the call-out siren, expressing extreme dissatisfaction of the present system of using an air-raid siren for the purpose of summoning firemen. The letter stated that it was the council's intention to pursue the subject in all available quarters with a view to having the existing system dispensed with.

Durham County Fire Brigade ranged from the rural areas in the west of the county to the heavily industrialised towns that bordered the banks of the rivers Tyne and Tees. Middlesbrough Fire Brigade, South Shields and Newcastle & Gateshead Joint Fire Service operated fireboats to which Durham contributed a portion of the costs. Much negotiating went on regarding the costs of maintaining and operating the boats, so much so that an initial failure to seek agreement with the Newcastle & Gateshead Joint Fire Service, and a threat by them to dispose of the boat in 1949, prompted Durham to consider acquiring the boat which would have meant an increase in the establishment of eight men at Hebburn to man the boat which would be moored on the river Tyne at Palmers Yard. Agreement was eventually reached whereby Durham would contribute one third of the operating costs of the boat, meaning that the plans for the county to operate its own boat were not proceeded with. This was the brigade's second attempt at acquiring a fireboat and a cadre of marine firefighters. At the inception of the brigade consideration was given to operating the Tees fireboat from a berth at Billingham, but in view of a suitable berth already provided on the south side of the river Tees the responsibility was ceded to Middlesbrough Fire Brigade.

Pending the arrival of new appliances, two Fordson hose layers were acquired from the Home Office, one for conversion into an emergency/foam salvage tender for Hebburn and the other into a hose carrier/general purpose lorry for Durham. The brigade workshops' staff and an outside contractor undertook these conversions. During the same period another conversion took place when the workshops' staff at Hebburn constructed a new canteen van using an old Austin ATV at a cost of £50. Durham County Fire Brigade was the first fire-fighting force in the north of England to have its own mobile canteen. It was equipped with calor gas heating and built-in water tanks that facilitated meals to be prepared whilst on the way to an incident. A similar vehicle was converted and rebuilt into a mobile control unit with both vehicles eventually giving over twenty years of service to the county brigade.

In August 1949, Murton Colliery Cooperative Society's warehouse and stables were destroyed by fire and the following month a Dutch barn containing sixty tons of straw was destroyed at Newlands Hall Farm, Frosterly. The same month a corrugated-iron building used as a cellulose store was destroyed at Dampney's Britannic Paint Works, Bill Quay, Hebburn.

Towards the end of the year radio equipment was introduced into the brigade, increasing the efficiency of appliance mobilisation quite dramatically. The scheme was based on a shared system with the police – initially for a twelve-month trial period – and six cars, eighteen appliances, plus an appliance at each of the mines' rescue brigades were equipped with the two-way radio equipment. Fixed transmitting and receiving equipment was installed in the control rooms at the Sands, Durham, 'B' Division Headquarters, Hebburn, and 'C' Division Headquarters at Stockton.

In November 1949, recruitment for the Auxiliary Fire Service (AFS) opened which entailed a considerable amount of work for some of the brigade's personnel. This illustrious organisation had its roots in the late 1930s when war seemed imminent; prompting the Government to

In the brigade's early history the Home Office Inspector of Fire Services, as well as a making an annual inspection of the brigade, was also treated to a parade and march past of the brigade's personnel and appliances. This march past was at the Sands, Durham City in 1949.

establish an emergency fire brigade organisation, for which a big recruiting campaign was started for volunteers to enrol in an auxiliary fire service. When war was declared in 1939 the auxiliary personnel were called up into full-time employment and later incorporated into the National Fire Service in 1941. After the cessation of hostilities the AFS and Civil Defence Corps were stood down.

Now there was an additional threat from Russia, in particular due to the development of atomic and hydrogen bombs, of which it was known from past experiences at the Japanese cities of Hiroshima and Nagasaki that the devastation caused by these bombs would be much more intensive than conventional arms. In order to adequately prepare for this perceived form of attack the Civil Defence and AFS was resurrected and every fire service in Britain was to recruit two auxiliaries for every whole-time fireman and one for every part-time fireman; 10 per cent of the numbers to be female. In Durham's case this equated to 1,090 auxiliaries. In the first recruiting drive, of the twenty people that applied, twelve were accepted including two females. Two wartime self-propelled pumps, three ATVs and twenty-four trailer pumps were issued on loan to the brigade from the Home Office Stores at Snaith for use by the AFS. Whole-time fire officer, Station Officer Ron Gatenby, was appointed to co-ordinate the activities of the AFS volunteers.

West Boldon Fire Station was closed on 30 August 1949 when agreement was reached for South Shields Fire Brigade to cover the Marsden and Whiteleas areas that were formerly covered by West Boldon, and for Sunderland Fire Brigade to provide cover to that part of Boldon Urban

There were many females within the ranks of the fire brigade, working in the control rooms and attached to the Auxiliary Fire Service. A number of them can be seen paraded before His Majesty's Inspector of Fire Services, the chief fire officer and members of the fire brigade committee.

District Council in which telephone calls were routed to Sunderland. The station was transferred to the county ambulance service that was already sharing part of the facilities. Ryhope was also closed when agreement was reached for the borough of Sunderland Fire Brigade to provide whole cover to the Ryhope area. No new fire stations had yet been constructed but the opportunity had been taken to try and at least secure suitable sites. The order of priority for the building program was: Durham City, where a new fire station and headquarters was proposed, then Bishop Auckland and lastly Wheatley Hill. A site earmarked for the new headquarters was located at the southern-most extreme of Aykley Heads. Sites were still being inspected for the proposed new fire stations but for the new headquarters the site at Aykley Heads was deemed not suitable and efforts were concentrated on looking at an alternative site at High Carr House Farm, Framwellgate Moor. Also this year all officers and firemen at Durham, Hebburn and Stockton were equipped with new helmets of the 'Middlesex' pattern, replacing the wartime tin helmets or 'battle bowlers' as they were known. The rest of the brigade's personnel received their issues during the following year. There was no standard pattern or style of fire helmet in the post-war years, each of the manufacturers having their own individual style, and it was possible for the observant fireman to tell which brigade a particular fireman came from by the style of helmet that was being worn.

During the county fire brigade's second year of existence the amount of calls dealt with had almost doubled to 2,240, of which 629 were for fires involving grass and gorse. In one day alone sixty-five calls were received. It was a particularly hot and dry summer, evident by the amount of calls to grass fires, and in addition to this there were ninety-eight occasions when appliances were turned out on special service calls to 'transport water during drought'!

The brigade workshop staff undertook many conversions of obsolete wartime appliances as illustrated here with Hebburn's Fordson emergency/foam tender and Durham's Austin canteen van. Both appliances gave over twenty years of service.

Hebburn's Fordson emergency/foam tender showing some of the specialised cutting and lighting equipment carried in the 1950s. An identical appliance was based at Billingham.

DURHAM COUNTY FIRE BRIGADE

AUXILIARY FIRE SERVICE

urgently requires

AUXILIARY FIREMEN & FIREWOMEN FOR YOUR LOCAL FIRE STATION TO WHICH YOU SHOULD APPLY. ENROLMENT FORMS AVAILABLE IN THEATRE FOYER.

Above: Various campaigns were undertaken in an effort to stimulate recruitment to the Auxiliary Fire Service, including the showing of recruitment films and displays in local cinemas. This poster was displayed in cinemas, supported by firemen attempting to spread the word.

Opposite: Graham's Timber Yard, Hebburn, was the scene of two large fires in short succession. Firemen are seen damping down at the first one in November 1949.

The work of the fire service carried on in the best traditions and during 1950 there were still plenty of fires requiring the services of the brigade. In June fire raged through a range of buildings containing plywood stores together with a number of timber stacks at Graham's Timber Yard, Hebburn. Five months later, on the eve of Guy Fawkes Night, the brigade was back again when £8,000 worth of damage was caused to a timber and corrugated-iron sawmill and timber storage shed. Hebburn was having a particular busy time. In May £80,000 worth of damage was caused to the Theatre Royal Cinema, Hebburn, and the living quarters of the adjoining Ellison Arms. Durham County Fire Brigade was supported by appliances from South Shields, Sunderland and Newcastle & Gateshead fire brigades and, owing to an acute water shortage, the South Shields fireboat was brought up to Hawthorn Leslie's shipyard to relay water to the fire. Occurring at 5.30 a.m., it took over two hours to bring the blaze under control; in all eleven pumps attended the call. On 13 August a clothing factory and the caretaker's house at Howden Bank, Lanchester, were severely damaged by fire.

Following a commendation for bravery by the King, Leading Fireman Henry Harris was additionally awarded the gallantry certificate of the Royal Humane Society in recognition of the brave attempt he made to rescue a fourteen-year-old boy from drowning in a quarry at Felling. The presentation was made by Mr M. Collingwood, chairman of Gateshead magistrates, in the presence of the assistant chief fire officer and members of the public. On arrival at the incident in question, Station Officer John Dale and Fireman J. Besford and Henry Harris, all stationed at Felling, leapt into a murky, rock-strewn pond at the bottom of a 110ft-deep quarry to save the boy from drowning. Diving deeply, Leading Fireman Harris found the boy trapped under a ledge and with some difficulty released the boy and brought him to the surface where the station officer and his crew administered artificial resuscitation, alas to no avail.

Recruitment campaigns to enhance the enrolment of volunteers into the Auxiliary Fire Service and other civil defence branches stepped up a pace in November with the brigade

Left: Leading Fireman Henry Harris was awarded a King's Commendation and a Royal Humane Society gallantry certificate in 1951 for his valiant attempts, with others, to rescue a young boy trapped in a water-filled quarry.

Opposite: One of Durham's fire officers publicly spreads the good word through the loudspeakers on the Mobile Recruiting appliance behind in an effort to encourage members of the public to enlist in the Auxiliary Fire Service.

participating in an extensive winter recruiting campaign, coinciding with a similar national campaign. The methods used to publicise the campaign were quite elaborate and intensive and included public displays of fire appliances – both ancient and modern – in principal towns in the brigade's area, fire prevention and civil defence public exhibitions, shop window displays of fire and civil defence equipment, the showing of recruitment slides at cinemas, public meetings, pre-recorded speeches broadcast by PA systems, posters advertising public displays of fire service, civil defence and police appliances and equipment, film shows and talks by fire service officers to private clubs, institutions, local organisations and trade councils, and recruitment talks in works canteens.

This was serious business. After all that the campaign resulted in the enrolment of sixty-four males and sixty-nine females, swelling the numbers in the brigade to ninety-eight and eighty-two respectively. There were not as many problems in recruiting applicants for appointment to the whole-time fire service, apart from the fact that one in four applicants failed to attain the required educational standard.

It was December 1950 when the first of four new water tenders were delivered, two from the Home Office Depot at Wakefield and two from James Whitson & Sons, coachbuilder of West Drayton, Middlesex. The Home Office examples were big appliances compared to those currently in service and featured 400-gallon water tanks and a carry-over from the wartime appliances – a demountable Coventry Climax pump at the rear, powered by its own petrol engine. A particular characteristic of these two appliances was the large searchlight mounted on a pole in front of the cab. One of them, issued to Bishop Auckland, came to grief not long after delivery when it overturned whilst en route to a fire. It was repaired and placed back into service. Apart from a single example delivered to Anglesey Fire Department in North

Wales, they were the sole examples of this particular style. The Whitson appliances were slightly smaller than the Home Office vehicles but had the same self-contained pumping equipment. Seventy of this style of appliance were built under Home Office central contract but they were the only two to operate in Durham. The new dual-purpose appliance with a 50ft wheeled escape ladder and 900gpm pump, ordered in 1948, was delivered from Dennis Bros, Guildford, in January 1951. This smart limousine appliance, powered by a Rolls-Royce eight-cylinder petrol engine, was assigned to Hebburn and operated as the first turnout appliance in that town for over twenty years. Owing to the delay in the supply of suitable chassis, more wartime appliances were converted or rebuilt in the brigade's own workshops under the supervision of Mr G.L. Strangeways, the transport officer. In 1951 a wartime Austin-Leyland appliance with separate pump was rebuilt into a smart limousine appliance with the 500gpm pump now driven from the road engine through a power take-off. A 120-gallon water tank was fitted and the hose reels enclosed in lockers with the main hose lockers covered by roller shutter lockers. Although homebuilt, the design was equivalent in quality to the appliances built by the leading fire engine manufacturers.

Another appliance constructed in the workshops was a new wireless/control vehicle. This appliance, formerly operating from Billingham, was converted for use as a mobile communications vehicle at large or prolonged incidents and operated for the next twenty years as such from Framwellgate Moor in the company of a similar canteen van that had undergone a previous conversion. The control unit was fitted with two-way wireless equipment, walkie-talkie master set, additional masts to enable wireless aerials to be raised to a height of 30ft in areas where radio reception was weak and two field telephones with sufficient cable, on reels to enable telephones to be operated at up to 2 miles distance from the van. The vehicle was characterised

Hebburn Fire Station was allocated this new Rolls-Royce-powered Dennis limousine appliance, complete with 50ft wheeled escape, in 1951. It operated from Hebburn Fire Station for its entire operational career of almost twenty years.

Two of these Whitson-bodied water tenders were delivered in December 1950. They featured 400-gallon water tanks, twin hose reels and the pump was a Coventry Climax type that could be easily removed and manhandled to a convenient water supply. The vehicle also towed a similar unit mounted on a trailer.

The shortage of new fire appliances prompted the brigade workshop, under the leadership of Transport Officer George Strangeways, to undertake conversions in-house. This former wartime Bedford vehicle was rebuilt into this smart limousine water tender.

by a clear glass red-and-white-chequered dome on the roof and similar chequered stripe alongside, universally signifying its role as a communications vehicle. A second Fordson hose-laying lorry was rebuilt into an emergency/foam salvage tender but because of the workload at the brigade workshops the contract for the conversion was awarded to Sherwood & Winn Ltd, of Newton Aycliffe. This appliance was allocated to Billingham.

Four further water tenders were ordered in 1951, two on semi-forward control Leyland Comet chassis and two on Dennis F8 chassis. Three bodybuilders applied for the contract of the Leyland Comets: Hampshire Car Bodies (HCB), Cumberland Coachworks and James Whitson & Sons. Cumberland Coachworks was discounted because, although their product seemed a good appliance, there were too many small lockers and the delivery schedule of eight to twelve months was uncertain. Whitson produced the most workmanlike appliance but their model was the costliest of the three and it was felt that this could not be justified; so HCB secured the contract at a price of £1,408, each with delivery in four months, provided some alterations could be made to the lockers and closed hose reel compartments could be fitted. Another two Commers were ordered at the same time, and this time six suppliers submitted tenders with the difference between the lowest and highest prices equalling over £1,000. For these appliances the tender for the chassis was awarded to Minories of Newcastle and a new company, Alfred Miles Ltd of Cheltenham, supplied the bodies. Miles was a post-war entrant into the fire service scene and had pioneered the use of light alloy in the construction of their fire appliances. It was not the cheapest tender but the combination of low, unladen weight and a 400-gallon water tank was the deciding factor in the purchase of these appliances. Hampshire Car Bodies was discounted

This is how the appliance looked before conversion. It started life as a 'heavy unit', one of hundreds of similar appliances hastily produced during the war. The pump was a self-contained unit with its own engine.

because it was felt that the design's light portable pump housed in an amidships locker took up too much space and the visibility from the cab was inferior to the Miles design. Delays in the delivery of the Dennis F8 appliances saw a further order being awarded to Miles for another three water tenders on Commer chassis. All in all, Durham operated a total of seven of these appliances. It can be seen that in the first three years of the brigade's existence standardisation was not possible owing to the limited availability of suitable chassis and long or uncertain delivery schedules. In this short period three different makes of chassis had been supplied: Commer, Dennis and Leyland; with bodies from four different coachbuilders: Home Office workshops, Dennis Bros, Alfred Miles and James Whitson.

His Majesty's Inspector of Fire Services, Mr Percy Booth OBE, returned to Durham in April 1951 for another annual inspection and exercise which was held at Usworth Aerodrome, Washington. He later witnessed a parade of 154 whole-time firemen at the Sands, Durham, after which a march past of personnel and a parade of ten appliances took place. Alderman J.W. Foster (chairman of the county council) presented the annual efficiency competition trophies to the respective fire station personnel. Mr Booth was accompanied throughout the inspection by Miss V.M. Garner, woman staff officer at the Home Office, the brigade's chief fire officer and officials of the county council. Assistant Chief Fire Officer Tozer commanded the parade. Lord Lawson, lord lieutenant of County Durham, visited the brigade training school during one of the passing out parades of new recruits and expressed 'how pleasing it was to see these well trained men, disciplined and ready at any moment, and the wonderful array of mechanical apparatus of the county's fire brigade'. He also commended the county council

This smart appliance started life as a pre-war lorry/mobile dam unit and was rebuilt in the brigade workshop into this mobile control unit. Based at Durham, it served for twenty years and is currently still in existence in the north-east of England, preserved in its operational condition.

Seven of these Miles-bodied Commer water tenders served in Durham, four of them later being converted into foam tenders. The aluminium construction and good cab visibility were big selling points of Miles fire engines.

on the efficient organisation of the brigade in the comparatively short time that the council had been a fire authority. Councillor J.R. Coxon, chairman of the fire brigade committee, also gave a speech stating, 'While personnel and equipment were second to none, the stations generally were not fit for so good a brigade'.

In July 1951 an early morning fire caused £15,000 damage to a range of two-storey buildings that included a chemical works, rope works and retail drapers at Messrs Finlaysons' factory, Nelson Road, Stockton. Eight pumps attended this incident. In September a fire involving three two-storey houses at Granville Terrace, Binchester, between Bishop Auckland and Spennymoor, required the attendance of five pumps. Four people escaped from the premises but unfortunately one female adult and one nine-year-old boy succumbed. During the same month a fire on the steamship *Bransfield* at Palmers shipyard, Hebburn, was attended to by eight pumps. This vessel, a whale meat ship, was seen to be on fire shortly after midnight on 19 September and prompted the start of a long and difficult operation that lasted until the following afternoon. The incident was one that required the combined efforts of firemen from Durham, Newcastle & Gateshead, South Shields and Sunderland fire brigades as well as those of the shipyard brigade. On the arrival of the first fire crews from Hebburn dense volumes of acrid smoke from burning dunnage and cork insulation were belching from the affected hold. As thousands of gallons of water were poured into the ship a severe list

A parade of appliances at the Sands, Durham, in 1952. The first appliance, from Wheatley Hill, is one of the wartime auxiliary towing vehicles that underwent a conversion to house the ladder in an enclosed box, in order to reduce the headroom so that it could fit into the appliance room. A similar vehicle served at Washington.

Mr Percy Booth, His Majesty's Inspector of Fire Services, and the chief fire officer inspect the ranks of firemen at one of the brigade's annual inspections. With three exceptions the men are still attired in wartime 'battle bowler' helmets.

developed that, by 3.34 a.m., had increased to twenty-two degrees to starboard. The ten jets of water that were in use at the time had to be reduced down to two and it was necessary to stop fire-fighting for long periods whilst employees at the yard drilled holes in the hull in order to release some of the water. Thereafter, major trailer pumps and salvage pumps were lowered into the holds and pumping out commenced. It was not until 1.57 p.m. on 22 September that the fire was finally extinguished. Eight pumps, emergency tender and a fireboat attended the incident. One week after the Bransfield fire, Stanley and Consett crews were called out to Southmoor golf course where a Royal Air Force Gloster Meteor jet aircraft from Middleton-St-George had crashed after exploding in mid-air over South Stanley. Three pumps and an emergency tender from Stanley, Consett and Hebburn attended this incident, together with a team of rescue workers from Louisa Colliery. The new walkie-talkie radios were put to good use during the incident. These early forms of communication were large ungainly pieces of equipment, housed in a backpack worn by the operator, a far cry from the small hand-held equipment commonplace now. The Coal Board firefighters that had provided cover to parts of the county of Durham since the pre-war days and continued to do so post-war in the Crook and Houghton-le-Spring areas were called out to a particularly tragic incident at 4.45 a.m.

Firemen at the training school undergo familiarisation with the hook ladder. With this ladder, working singly or in pairs, it was possible to scale the heights of most buildings from windowsill to windowsill.

on 29 May, following reports of an explosion at Easington Colliery. Appliances from Newcastle and both the Durham stations attended but the concerted rescue efforts were in vain and eighty-three miners aged between eighteen and sixty-eight years died in the 900ft-deep workings. As if this tragedy was not enough the incident was compounded even further by the deaths of two members of the colliery rescue teams who collapsed during the rescue operations.

Stockton Fire Brigade was busy towards the end of 1951. On 2 October five pumps and the foam tender attended a fire at Malleable Pipe Works, Portrack Lane, where a 50,000-cuft gasholder was involved in fire. On the 23rd, just before 2 a.m., the first and second floors of the four-storey Black Lion Hotel in High Street caught fire from which fifteen people had to be rescued by the brigade, six of them requiring hospitalisation. On 1 December the crews were back in the thick of things attending to a serious fire at Towers Warehouse, Bridge Street, where the upper floors and roof of a three-storey chemical warehouse were severely damaged by fire. Five pumps, emergency tender and turntable ladder were required at this fire before it was brought under control.

By 1952 sites were acquired for new fire stations at Middleton in Teesdale, Peterlee and Stanhope and the doors at Barnard Castle were raised to 10ft to permit the housing of the new types of appliances being introduced into the brigade. The new fire station at Peterlee was to be built in two stages. The first stage comprised the erection of four-appliance bays, two of which would be used for a dormitory and temporary office accommodation. The second stage would see the removal of the temporary accommodation so four appliances could be accommodated, the erection of a drill tower and the construction of an underground water tank. Unfortunately the actual construction of new premises could not yet go ahead because of restrictions imposed

Escape drills were also an essential part of the regime of the fireman's routine. Using a Merryweather 50ft all-steel wheeled escape, recruit firemen at Felling get to work running hose up to the first floor of the scaffold drill tower.

by the Government. Although the brigade was actively seeking new sites, notably for the new headquarters, the actual proposed building plan was declined by the Home Office unless the amount of steel used in the construction was reduced from eighteen tons to fifteen tons. Hartlepool gained a second appliance when premises across the road from the fire station were acquired to house the new addition; there were now two fire stations opposite one another. At Stanley an extension to increase the accommodation for the personnel by the addition of a second floor was gaining completion. Wheatley Hill firemen, previously accommodated in property described as being in immediate danger of collapse and in need of urgent replacement, moved into a new temporary fire station in Quetlaw Road. The new premises consisted of a large corrugated-iron aircraft hangar-type of building painted black but, in order to make it appear more presentable, a brick façade was added to the front shrewdly camouflaging the basic construction of the station. This temporary fire station lasted for over thirty years.

Both Leyland Comet water tenders were in service by the end of the year, the first one going to Hebburn and the second to Stockton. One of the Comets was later fitted with a spring-loaded ladder gallows assembly housing a new type of Merryweather all-alloy 45ft ladder, an item of equipment that was designed as a replacement for the wheeled escape ladder. Although no other examples of this ladder were adopted by Durham County Fire Brigade it was indeed the precursor of other developments and did lead to the eventual replacement of the wheeled escape but not for another twenty-five years. Apart from the pre-war appliances, the Leyland Comets were the first post-war appliances in the county to have built-in main pumps powered from the road engine, although all of the pre-war appliances were equipped with this facility.

Stanley Fire Station was one of only two county council fire stations that had been purpose built before the establishment of the NFS and the county fire brigade. The two-storey extension to the left was a post-war addition to afford the firemen better accommodation facilities.

Wheatley Hill's temporary replacement fire station at Quetlaw Road, erected in 1952, was simply a corrugated-iron shed, enhanced by a brick façade. It remained in use until 1989.

Opposite: Stockton's turntable ladder in use at a water tower at Towers Warehouse, Stockton-on-Tees, on 1 December 1951. Firemen can be seen gaining entry into the second floor by means of a wheeled escape.

The urgent need for replacement at Wheatley Hill was evident by this photograph of the original Wolmerhausen Street accommodation, which was described by the chief fire officer as being 'in immediate danger of collapse'.

The wartime appliances and the four previously delivered Commers all had separate, self-contained pumps powered by their own engine, separate from the road engine. The arrival of the new appliances meant the gradual replacement and disposal of the pre-war and post-war vehicles although it was many years before the fleet was completely modernised.

Weardale Rural District Council expressed concern at the fire protection available in the district and suggested that it would be better served by the establishment of a retained fire station at St John's Chapel together with the provision of fire extinguishers in suitable places for public use. In response to these concerns a complete survey of the district was undertaken and a test call was placed to the retained unit at Stanhope. The appliance was in attendance at St John's Chapel within twenty minutes and at Wearhead in a further two minutes proving that the fire authority were meeting its obligations regarding the attendance times to rural areas. However, in order to allay the concerns of the council a box containing six lengths of hose, branch pipe, standpipe, bar and key, two buckets and two fire extinguishers was provided at St John's Chapel and both Wearhead and Rookhope were given boxes, to be placed on a suitable wall containing one fire extinguisher, a stirrup pump and two buckets.

Early staff cars and utility vehicles for officers consisted of these Austin A40-types. One of these vans was based at Wheatley Hill for use by the part-time firemen to travel from the colliery where many of them worked on the same shift and could therefore all travel to the fire station together when required.

At 3 a.m. on 5 May, the Crook Mines rescue men were initially turned out to Hamsterley Forest where fire engulfed 300 acres of woodland. One hundred military personnel aided the twelve fire crews at this incident. In March the following year the military were once again called in to assist the fire brigade when a 'controlled' fire got out of hand at Egglestone Moor during high winds and eventually destroyed 10 acres of heather and scrub. Also in March, the new canteen van was sent to Newcastle where the Newcastle & Gateshead Joint Fire Service were attending a prolonged warehouse fire on the Quayside. Until South Shields Fire Brigade bought their own canteen van in 1965, the Durham vehicle was the only one in the region and was available for use with any of the region's fire brigades, provided that the operating costs were met by the requesting authority.

Recruitment of AFS personnel was an ongoing commitment and was enhanced by frequent displays throughout the county. Displays were held at agricultural shows at Hebburn, Consett and Stanley, and frequently displays of fire appliances were set up in town centres, notably at Bishop Auckland, Crook, Stockton, Washington and Willington. A small but successful door-to-door campaign resulted in the total strength increasing to 146 males and 106 females. Of all the recruiting methods tried, door-to-door canvassing was the most effective but the position still remained unsatisfactory. One particular door-to-door canvas in Spennymoor resulted in the enrolment of just one new recruit. The biggest training exercise to have occurred in the north-east since the war took place on 25 March when Durham's ancient castle was 'incendiary bombed'.

Directed by Chief Fire Officer C.V. Hall the exercise, devised to test mobilising arrangements throughout the area and boost AFS recruitment and training, simulated scattered air raids on Tyneside culminating in a bomb attack on Durham City. Over 200 AFS personnel from Durham, Darlington, Middlesbrough, Newcastle & Gateshead, North Riding of Yorkshire, South Shields, Sunderland and Tynemouth attended with a total of twenty-five fire appliances. Walkie-talkie radio sets were used on inter-fire ground control, operated by AFS women who also staffed the brigade's canteen van. As well as frequent training exercises and weekly drill nights, many efforts were expended in creating a rewarding social life for the AFS volunteers, one example being regular Scottish and Scandinavian dancing classes at various fire stations that were organised by the brigade's senior woman officer. These events were also supported by the whole-time and retained personnel. The brigade anticipated that its revised target of 1,140 AFS members would have been reached by this time but this prediction was far from the truth and in fact was never attained.

The county's biggest fire to date occurred the day after Bonfire Night 1952, during 70mph gales and a 'terrific rainstorm' when twenty-four appliances, including those from the Mines Rescue Brigade, were mobilised to a pitch blending plant at Thristlington Coke Works where sixteen pitch beds containing 3,000 tons of pitch were alight. The fire involved the whole plant including several six-storey brick-built stills, condensers, tanks of naphtha and railway wagons, with the flames being visible from a distance of 20 miles away. An attack using foam was

One of the two Leyland Comet appliances, the first new appliances in the county to feature built-in pumps. This one was fitted with a Merryweather 45ft light alloy extension ladder, the precursor to the modern Lacon 464 ladder.

Recruitment campaigns for the AFS were elaborate affairs and consisted of displays of appliances through the ages as illustrated in this scene. With one exception, all of the appliances in this December 1950 photograph are from the pre-war era.

hampered by the high winds and eventually thirteen jets of water were used before the blaze was brought under control. Damage was estimated at £250,000. Another fire occurred at the plant in November 1954 when five pumps attended a fire in a disused still and workshop. A bit further a-field, 1953 was a bad one for the citizens of the low-lying counties of Essex, Lincolnshire, Norfolk and Suffolk where a combination of extremely high tides and strong winds on the night of 31 December created a powerful storm surge resulting in a tide 9ft higher than predicted causing flooding of an area in excess of 160,000 acres of land. During the disaster 307 people drowned, 24,000 homes were flooded and 46,000 livestock were lost. Despite gallant efforts by the local emergency services and volunteers the disaster was, by the nature of its severity, completely outside the capabilities of the normal resources. On 11 February, Chief Fire Officer Hall was asked by the Home Office to organise a relief contingent for Operation 'Seawall', comprising personnel and appliances from twelve northern fire brigades to assist the beleaguered people in the flooded areas.

Ninety-nine officers and men were hastily assembled with a total of thirty-three vehicles departing in convoy under the command of Deputy Chief Fire Officer Tozer. Durham's contribution was two officers, twenty-two other ranks (all volunteers) and five pumps, the canteen van, a mobile repair vehicle and one each of towing vehicle, car and motorcycle. On arrival the crews were engaged in pumping and salvage work in the Mablethorpe and Sutton on Sea areas. They returned to the county on 19 February. The north-east also suffered from the adverse conditions, fortunately not to the great extent of the Anglia-region. Billingham suffered serious flooding at the beginning of the year and on 31 January industrial and residential properties in the Portrack, Haverton Hill and Port Clarence districts were flooded up to a depth of 4ft in places over a 5 square mile area when the river Tees broke its banks in three places causing floodwater to enter over 400 houses. The fire brigade were engaged for seven days committing forty-seven vehicles and appliances to the incident. Man's other enemy – fire – continued unabated.

In March 1953 the entire circle, projection rooms and the main roof of the 1937-built, 1,200-seat Plaza Cinema at Blaydon were destroyed by fire. Twelve appliances, including a turntable ladder from Durham County, supported by appliances from Northumberland and Newcastle & Gateshead fire brigades, attended the early morning blaze which could be seen by responding crews from over 2 miles away. The fire was brought under control within just one hour and, according to Chief Fire Office Hall who took command of the operations, this was the quickest

In the early 1950s there were many joint AFS exercises held in the north-eastern region. Here a selection of pre-war, wartime and one post-war appliances from the retained and whole-time divisions gather at the assembly point of one such exercise.

dealt with major cinema fire he had ever known. So much water had collected in the front stalls that when firemen burst open an emergency exit a 3ft wall of water surged into the street scattering the crews and bystanders. In the best traditions of the brigade 'Tabby', the cinema cat, was found alive and well in the basement and removed to a place of safety. Four days after the cinema fire and also at Blaydon, the kitchen, dining hall and cellulose polishing shop at Northern Bedding Companies premises, Derwenthaugh, were severely damaged. Langley Park's retained crew had a rude awakening when they responded to the Kings Cinema in the town on 22 March. Ten pumps and a turntable ladder could not prevent the whole of the contents of the building being destroyed. Six days later, eleven appliances and crews, aided by 100 armed forces personnel, tackled a heath fire at Edmundbyers Fell where 12 square miles of heather were burnt when controlled burning got out of hand due to high winds. On 5 May Hebburn's crews tackled a chemical fire at Morganite Resistors, Bede Trading Estate, Jarrow, where the product Cadmium was involved. All the crews had to be attired in breathing apparatus and undertake medical examinations afterwards. Apparently there had only been two fires in the whole of the country involving Cadmium. In June the clock tower at Lumley Castle succumbed to a fire to which four pumps and Durham's turntable ladder attended.

Auxiliary Fire Service exercises were held in October at Tharsis Copper Works, Hebburn, and ICI Works at Billingham. Additionally, the service attended other exercises in conjunction with AFS personnel in other brigade areas. Exercise 'Arbiei' at South Shields was attended by six appliances manned by AFS and retained personnel and, two days later, exercise 'Seahorse' at Newcastle saw six AFS appliances attend. At the time the appliances allocated to the AFS were wartime standard appliances, but expected in January were eight brand new Bedford 'atomic fire engines', the famous green goddesses.

The two Dennis F8 water tenders were delivered in August. These were basically smaller versions of the new dual-purpose appliance at Hebburn but featured smaller 120hp six-cylinder Rolls-Royce engines and 500gpm rear-mounted pumps. Originally known as the 'Ulster' model having been designed originally for the Northern Ireland fire authority – these appliances were only 6ft 6in wide. They were initially assigned to Bishop Auckland and Hebburn, but no more of this style were ordered although three further F8 chassis were delivered with bodywork by Alfred Miles, a company that was awarded many further contracts over the succeeding years until it merged with Dennis Bros and faded into oblivion. Towards the end of the year St Paul's Church, Spennymoor, was the scene of a ten-pump fire and, in October, just after midnight, six pumps attended the Eldon Brick Works, Eldon, where damage amounting to £4,000 occurred at the company's garage, workshops and builders' stores that contained fourteen motor vehicles. Two further fires of note occurred in November. The first was another blaze at Towers Chemical Warehouse, Stockton, on the 17th of the month where eight pumps attended, whilst on the 28th twelve pumps were turned out to Grays Central Shipyard, Hartlepool where £7,000 of damage was caused to a frame shop.

To end 1953 on a pleasant note, half of the new Peterlee Fire Station opened on 31 October and Horden Fire Station was closed. The fire station at Peterlee was being built in two stages, with the first stage comprising the appliance room block, whereby the two centre bays were occupied by fire engines and the two outer bays used as living accommodation. When the second stage of building commenced a new accommodation block was constructed and the garage became one of four bays. At Middleton in Teesdale a larger appliance room was provided together with a recreation and lecture room whilst at Stanley the firemen built their own drill tower. Firemen C. Rowe and A.K. Wall from Barnard Castle received commendations for their rescue of a woman marooned in the river Tees during August. Rowe entered the river on four separate occasions and swam out three times with a rope but each time was carried away by the flood.

There is no limit to the extent that the county's firemen will go to attain adequate water supplies. Assistant Chief Fire Officer Tozer supervises the siting of a Sigmund-Morris light trailer pump in the North Sea during an exercise at Crimdon Dene in the 1950s.

On the fourth attempt he assisted an Army officer who eventually affected the rescue. Walls took an active part in the rescue and artificial respiration and organised the removal of the casualty. Fireman Rowe was later awarded the Royal Humane Society's Testimony on Vellum. In May further commendations were awarded: Firemen F.E. Jones and A. Stainsby from Durham City station received the National Canine Defence League's silver medal and a bronze medal and citation certificate from the RSPCA for their rescue of a dog from a derelict pit shaft at Hetton-le-Hole on the last day of May. The chief fire officer received the British Empire Medal. He also received, together with eight other officers and men, the Coronation Medal.

Two schools were severely damaged by fire in January 1954: Alderman Wraith Grammar School in Stanley and St Peter's School, Jarrow. On the 24th and 25th of the same month the brigade sent reinforcements to the North Riding of Yorkshire when the Cleveland Flour Mills at Thornaby on Tees were destroyed by fire. Stanley Fire Station had an interesting call in February: to the station's watchroom where a wastepaper basket, armchair and desk were partially burned. On 10 April, ten pumps attended a fire at Mellanby's Warehouse, Quayside, Stockton, at which £16,000 worth of damage was caused. Earlier in the month the brigade's own training school at Felling became a statistic when one length of hose, eleven mattresses and two salvage sheets were destroyed in a fire in a hose cabinet. In August, Durham County Fire Brigade was once again called to assist West Hartlepool Fire Brigade when ten county appliances were despatched to assist in a major fire in a multi-storey warehouse used for the manufacture of matches in one of the enclosed dock systems. Considerable discussions over many years occurred between West Hartlepool Fire Brigade and Durham County Fire Brigade regarding the provision of fire cover between West Hartlepool and Durham's Hartlepool Fire Station in the days before

The first new fire station to be built in Durham was at Peterlee, built in two stages. The accommodation in the two end bays was only temporary and when stage two of the construction program commenced these two areas became additional appliance bays.

centralised mobilising occurred. West Hartlepool Corporation – that received and called out the Durham contingent on occasions – was reluctant to accept responsibility for receiving fire calls or sounding the siren or call bells for Hartlepool's retained firemen. It was felt that to rely on fires in the area being dealt with satisfactorily by a part-time brigade was an unjust risk where it was believed the public and the person making fire calls from the borough of Hartlepool would not fully understand the legal position governing the responsibility for attendance at fires, and would blame West Hartlepool Fire Brigade if an early and adequate attendance at fires was not made. Many of the attendances to fires in the Hartlepool and West Hartlepool district were joint turnouts and in some places one brigade could cover more effectively than the other with a financial adjustment of the running costs; but obtaining a satisfactory compromise was a complex affair. The matter persisted for many years with correspondence and meetings between the boroughs and the Home Office never coming to agreement. Unknown at the time, the matter would be resolved in the future, but in a way that no one could yet foresee.

Recruitment of whole-time and retained firemen was a continual process with a constant turnover of operational staff. Industries were working to full capacity and expanding, and many firemen – not happy with the conditions, pay and working hours – left the fire brigade to seek better remuneration elsewhere. Hence, at the Felling Training School recruits' courses were run continuously, especially considering the areas from where the recruits were drafted, from which, as well as the north-eastern brigades, included Cumberland, Carlisle and Westmorland. Mr H.N. Davison was appointed as commandant in May 1952. One fireman not happy with the prevailing conditions was T.F. (Fred) Elton who resigned in June 1954 to take up employment with the British Oxygen Co. where there were apparently excellent prospects for advancement.

Mellanby's warehouse at Stockton-on-Tees was gutted by fire in 1954. Stockton's Merryweather turntable ladder is used to assess the structural damage to what looks like a precarious, unsupported gable end.

As happened with several others, things did not work out as well as expected and Elton applied for and was reinstated in the brigade. This was a wise decision because he later became the commandant of the training school, aspiring to command the county fire brigade as chief fire officer before moving across the river Tyne to take command of the Tyne & Wear Metropolitan Fire Brigade.

As the years progressed the number of calls to the brigade steadily increased. More large fires occurred towards the end of 1954. On 11 November an early morning fire at the six-storey Corporation Warehouse, Stockton-on-Tees was attended by twenty appliances, on the 17th the oil works at ICI Billingham needed thirteen appliances for a fire in two Benzine stores and on 8 December ten pumps were needed to tackle severe flooding in Lanchester Village when 8 acres of land was flooded to a depth of 3ft. The Stockton Corporation Warehouse, situated in Silver Street, comprised of six stories containing rubber tyres, sacks, fertiliser chemicals and industrial powdered soap. The first indication of fire was seen at 3.20 a.m. by a patrolling policeman on the opposite bank of the river. At about the same time the wharf night watchman saw a glow and noticed that the second-floor loading door at the east end of the building was burning. By the time the first appliances from Stockton arrived flames were coming from the windows on all floors at the building's east end. As the fire progressed most of the floors collapsed and the roof fell in. A particular hazard here was fumes from the chemical Cymag. Residential properties in the area were evacuated and all personnel warned of the dangerous atmosphere. Firemen wearing breathing apparatus worked in relays under difficult and dangerous conditions for some considerable time removing Cymag and damping down. Sixteen pumps, three turntable ladders and the Tees' fireboat were in attendance and in all twenty-two jets were in operation. This was the county's biggest fire to date.

The district mobilising scheme was initiated for the first time in December when Sunderland Fire Brigade was faced with its biggest peacetime fire: Joplings Department Store in High Street West was gutted by fire. In accordance with previous agreements Durham County Fire Brigade's control room co-ordinated the reinforcing moves which not only included despatching appliances to the fire but also the organisation of appliances to standby at a depleted fire station. Twenty pumps were mobilised to the incident from as far away as Northumberland and the brigade's canteen van was in attendance at the fire for five hours providing a valuable service to the hard-pressed crews. During the period April 1953 to April 1954, the brigade attended a total of 1,957 calls of which 199 were false alarms either of malicious origin or made with good intent. As had been the case over the previous seven years of Durham County Fire Brigade's existence Stockton was the busiest with 243 calls, thirty-one of them being false alarms; Hebburn was second, another foregone conclusion and third was Billingham. Houghton-le-Spring was the least busy whole-time station with a total of seventy calls, whilst the busiest retained station was Hartlepool with seventy calls, followed by Washington with forty. Chopwell was only called out on three occasions and Middleton in Teesdale twice. The wireless scheme, previously divided into three main transmitting and receiving sites at Durham, Hebburn and Stockton was centralised in 1954; the fixed receivers were removed from Hebburn and Stockton and all wireless traffic thereafter was routed to the central brigade control at the Sands, Durham.

An annual display and drill competition was inaugurated in 1954, an event that was seen as one of public interest and value and a useful factor in maintaining good relationships between the county council and other local authority and industrial brigades. Usually held at the County School of Agriculture at Houghall, the event provided an ideal venue for recruitment for the AFS considering the crowd of 4,000 members of the public that usually attended the events. At the inaugural event seven local authority and twelve industrial fire brigades competed.

Wheatley Hill Fire Station's team were victors in the annual National Fire Brigades' Quiz Competition, the finals of which were held at the Fire Service Staff College, Dorking, Surrey.

Stockton Fire Station personnel were victors in three of the events and Bishop Auckland in two events. In an effort to step up the campaign for recruitment several mobile fire-recruiting units operated throughout the country and fire officers continued with their talks in factory canteens and public gatherings. Whenever local cinemas had the occasion to show a civil defence film, display tables were set up in the foyer manned by fire service personnel intent on encouraging cinemagoers to enrol in the AFS. Every year brigade quiz competitions were organised nationally with local heats taking place leading up to a national semi-final and final competition. A team from Wheatley Hill was successful in gaining first place in the 1955 national final.

The three Miles-bodied Dennis F8 appliances were delivered in mid-1955 and went operational at Billingham, Durham and Peterlee. Ordered for the next year were two new types of appliances for the Durham fleet, specifically for the retained stations where a requirement was that the appliances should be no more than 7ft 2in wide. There was now plenty of availability and choice of vehicles, so two appliances were ordered from Miles, on Bedford chassis and two from Carmichael & Sons of Worcester on Karrier chassis. The Karriers were ordered for stations in hilly areas because of their greater brake horsepower and the Bedfords for stations with less hilly areas.

Regarding new premises, improvements were still restricted by Governmental limitations of capital expenditures but the construction of Bishop Auckland's new fire station had started and AFS garages were built at Felling, Hebburn, Dunston and Seaham to house the new green goddesses. Two old wartime towing vehicles and eight trailer pumps, now obsolete, were returned to the Home Office Stores at Tranwell, Morpeth.

In 1955 the National Coal Board's Fire and Rescue Brigade at Crook that provided cover for the county on a contractual basis was the first unit in attendance when the Cooperative

One of the two Karrier Gamecock water tenders delivered in 1956. This appliance and its sister operated as a pair for many years from Wheatley Hill. (I. Moore)

Society's three-storey premises in the town suffered a major fire on 20 April that required a total attendance of ten pumps. The Coal Board provided a valuable and economical service to the county, providing whole-time cover to Crook and the surrounding districts as did a sister station at Houghton-le-Spring. In May, Vaux's Brewery, Bridge Road, Stockton, was severely damaged by fire at which eight pumps were required. However, in November an even bigger brewery fire occurred. Peterlee's crews were first alerted at just before 6 a.m. when Nimmo's Brewery at Castle Eden Dene was reported to be on fire. On arrival it was found that a large range of buildings at the rear used as a maltings was well alight with part of the roof collapsed and the fire spreading rapidly to other areas of the site. Additional appliances were immediately ordered and, upon the arrival of both the chief and the assistant chief fire officers, pumps were made up to fifteen and the turntable ladder and control unit ordered on. By the time the fire had been extinguished most of the contents of beer in casks and one million bottles of beer in wooden and metal alloy crates were destroyed in the blaze. Fire-fighting on the lower floors was hampered by the descent of some 450 tons of barley from the second floor, which collapsed during the height of the fire. Crews were engaged at this fire for four days dealing with the lengthy and laborious task of removing the barley and extinguishing small pockets of fire. Just weeks after the Crook Cooperative Society fire that was attended in the first instance by the Crook Mines Rescue Brigade, notice was given that from 8 a.m. on 11 July the Coal Board would no longer attend fires for the county or surface fires at the brigade's colliery premises in both Northumberland and Durham. Negotiations with the Coal Board and the union failed to resolve the matter, other than formally granting three months' notice, and on 30 November the Coal Board's firemen withdrew from their obligations to fight fires. Emergency fire stations had to be established in the areas now deprived of cover and, initially, temporary accommodation was provided at Houghton-le-Spring's superintendent's police station and an old Ministry of Works' food office at Crook. There was not enough time to recruit additional personnel for the stations over and above the normal establishment, so the stations were manned with whole-time personnel by taking an appliance out of service at Stockton and Hebburn or reducing the manning at other stations. The occupation at the police station was short-lived and the appliance and personnel were transferred to the children's home, Houghton-le-Spring, rented on an annual tenancy after operating for a short time from Millhayes House, Park View, Hetton-le-Hole. The Coal Board's problems prompted a review of the establishment scheme and suggested, amongst other things, the setting up of four divisions instead of the present three and the replacement of Felling and Hebburn by a single new fire station, a new fire station between Chester-le-Street and Houghton-le-Spring, a new station at Stockton to replace both Billingham and Stockton and the closure of Ferryhill resulting in a reduction of four appliances from the present strength. Most of the proposals came to fruition except the closing of Ferryhill although it did close many years later for different reasons. The new divisions saw the addition of 'D' Division, which consisted of five stations, Spennymoor, Bishop Auckland, Barnard Castle, Middleton in Teesdale and Stanhope taken from the original 'A' Division with the divisional headquarters being situated at Bishop Auckland. In charge of 'A' Division was J.W. Stonehouse; W.Y. Hagan commanded 'B' Division, J.W. Smith 'C' Division and J. Clazey 'D' Division. During the year seventeen lives were lost by fire, four of them children, all except one succumbing to severe burns caused by clothing being accidentally ignited by open fires. The most common cause of loss of life from fire in this era was open, unguarded fires where items of clothing such as long nightdresses were ignited through the wearer coming into close contact with an open fire grate. Over the succeeding years, owing to intense fire safety publicity and the decrease of coal fires – replaced by central heating systems – these types of incidents have fortunately become almost non-existent.

The year of 1956 got off to a bad start. The divisional officer of the Hebburn division since the formation of the county fire authority, Edmund Claude Waters, died in hospital in early January at the tender age of forty-nine years. Formerly the chief fire officer of West Hartlepool Fire Brigade from 1937 to 1941, his career started in 1931 as a fireman mechanic with the Cambridge Borough Police Fire Brigade from where he transferred to Enfield UDC Fire Brigade and later to the borough of Wood Green, Middlesex where, in 1937 he became deputy chief fire officer. In the following year he secured the position of chief fire officer in the county borough of West Hartlepool. In the years leading up to the nationalisation of the fire services he was responsible for the setting up of the Emergency Fire Brigades' Organisation in the Hartlepool area and the Teesside Mutual Aid Scheme. During the reign of the National Fire Service he attained the rank of company officer and thereafter, on the return of fire services to local authority control, despite expressing a preference to remain in the West Hartlepool area he was appointed to the post of divisional officer in the Durham County Fire Brigade.

Esh Winning's Pavilion Cinema suffered a major fire in January 1956 and one month later ten pumps were called to Eldon School, Eldon. On 19 February the county's district mobilising scheme, set up in March 1951 following the West Hartlepool timber yard fire, was initiated again when Sunderland Fire Brigade called for assistance whilst fighting a large fire at Grantham's Furniture Store in the town centre. This fire occurred at 9.30 p.m. during a bitterly cold night when water froze in the hoses putting some of them out of action. Chief Fire Officer Allison of Sunderland Fire Brigade paid tribute to the firemen for the way they had stood up to the intense cold and he had a special word of praise for the part-time volunteers who had come in from the

William Hagan, divisional officer, commanded the brigade's 'B' Division and was later promoted to the position of assistant chief fire officer upon the retirement of Charles Tozer.

county to assist the Sunderland Brigade. Durham's contribution during this fire was eight pumps and the canteen van. So good was the working relationship between Sunderland and Durham fire brigades that proposals were made in 1955 to merge the two authorities. In November the chief fire officer's post had become vacant and it was suggested by the Home Office that before the vacant post was filled consideration should be given to the possibility of combining the areas served by Sunderland and Durham County brigades. The Sunderland Watch Committee rejected the suggestion and both fire brigades retained their separate entities.

The building replacement program was making good progress. The first stage of Bishop Auckland's new station on Watling Road was occupied in May 1956 and the old premises handed back to United Automobile Services from whom the garages were leased; construction was authorised for the new Spennymoor station and a new fire station at Fencehouses, to replace both Chester-le-Street and the temporary fire station at Houghton-le-Spring was approved. However having found a suitable site at Woodrow, Fencehouses, the county council was informed by the Secretary of State that on the information received the proposed site appeared to fall within the terms of a general embargo on fire station building and should be deferred temporarily. Washington received a full-sized water tender in place of its converted towing vehicle following the extension of the garage and incorporation of a new recreation room at the Spout Lane premises. Four new appliances were received: two Miles-bodied Bedfords, one for Hartlepool and the other for Langley Park, and two Karrier Carmichael water tenders. The two Bedfords, of semi-forward control configuration, were the only ones of this particular type to serve in Durham but led the way for several other batches of forward control Bedford Miles water tenders and water tender-escapes that served the county for many years.

The new fire station at Bishop Auckland was also built in two stages and is pictured here after the completion of the first phase. The town's pre-war Dennis Light 4 appliance, named *Aclet*, accompanies a wartime Fordson escape-carrying unit and a new Dennis F8 water tender.

The new Hartlepool Bedford remained in the town for its entire career whilst the Langley Park example was later relocated to Washington. The two Karriers with bodywork by Carmichael & Sons of Worcester and 500gpm Gwynne pumps were based on the Gamecock chassis and were advertised in company literature as being shorter, narrower and lighter than any other appliance of the time. The top speed was rated at over 60mph and acceleration rates from 0 to 40mph in 22 seconds was said to be superior to many other appliances. These first two, of a total of seven Karriers, operated from Wheatley Hill as a matched pair for many years. More new appliances were issued on loan to the county's AFS to join the previously delivered green goddesses. Now the AFS had a communications unit, control unit, pipe carrier, three Land Rovers and a motorcycle.

More recruiting displays occurred with events held during 1955 at Bishop Auckland, Billingham, Stanley and Hebburn Show. In the following year an interesting Transportable Water Unit (Bikini Unit) was added to the fleet. This was an appliance that carried inflatable rafts and nine portable pumps and in common with the rest of the post-war AFS fleet was finished in an olive green livery. The rubber bikini rafts were stowed in canvas bags and could be readily inflated and lowered into the water, whereupon one of the Coventry-Climax portable pumps was used as the power unit giving the craft a speed of up to six knots. There were only three of these units in the north east, the Durham one being the first. The total of AFS personnel now numbered 293 males and 110 females but had decreased by eighty-six due to the weeding out of 'ineffectives'. The

Washington Fire Station in 1949, showing the call-out siren and the rudimentary framework where hoses were hauled up for drying. In 1956 the garages were rebuilt in order to accommodate a conventional-sized fire engine.

biggest contingent served at Hebburn, thirty-five personnel, and Peterlee with twenty-seven. An interesting combined Civil Defence and AFS large-scale exercise took place at Jarrow in October 1957 during which ten old houses were set on fire to provide a realistic training environment.

Leading Fireman J. Fiddaman from Consett was commended this year for the rescue of a dog from a disused mineshaft at Edmunbyers. With the aid of his colleagues he allowed himself to be lowered by rope down an 80ft-deep shaft where the dog was recovered safely from running water at the bottom. In August 1957 another dog was rescued from a cliff ledge at Ryhope, 25ft from the top of a 100ft cliff. Leading fireman J. Rodgers of Seaham was commended for the part he played in the rescue. There is no doubt that a dog's best friend was man and in Durham's case it was the fireman. Less glamorous special service calls at the time included one where the brigade were called to remove a swarm of bees from the council offices, watering newly sown fields during drought and on three occasions crews were called to remove persons trapped by fingers in windows.

The turnover of staff and consequent recruitment to replace vacancies was a continual process and in November 1956 another previously resigned fireman was reinstated to the nominal roll. Fireman Eric Whaley had resigned after six years' service to take up a post with the City of Salisbury Fire Brigade in Rhodesia but the unavailability of suitable housing for his family prompted a return to the United Kingdom some twelve months later. He remained in the county fire brigade and ended his fire-fighting career with the rank of divisional officer.

Durham was the first of the northern brigades to be assigned one of the new AFS Commer transportable water units (bikini units), which carried three inflatable rafts and nine portable pumps. One of the rafts, contained in a canvas bag, is seen being offloaded here.

Interesting fires in 1956 were those at the ICI Oil Works, Billingham in November to which ten pumps were despatched. The brigade was back there one month later when the carbon-dioxide (CO_2) plant caught fire, and returned on the last day of 1957 when the CO_2 plant caught fire again. Eight pumps attended this one. A fire at Hudson's Timber Yard, Moat Street, Stockton on the penultimate day of the year was fought with the aid of six pumps. There were several other large fires where five or more pumps attended, including Pyman & Bell's Timber Yard, Durham in May, Coundon Station Timber Yard, also in May, Weardale Coke Works, Spennymoor and forest fires at Hell Hole Woods in June and Ropers Wood, Hurworth Burn in May.

The strive for new and improved premises continued unabated and at the beginning of 1957 the erection of Spennymoor's new fire station at Queen Street was well underway and the occupation of the new headquarters at Framwellgate Moor was imminent. The town of Aycliffe, under development as a new town, featured in the brigade's original establishment plan but was deferred until an appropriate number of houses were built for the firemen to reside in, within easy reach of the station. The manning here was to be on a day manning system where whole-time firemen were employed during the day with the same men being available to respond to the station from their homes in the evenings and at night. A site at Central Avenue was inspected for this station. In Stockton a site was inspected at South Road, Norton, and for Dunston's replacement a seemingly suitable site at Market Lane, opposite Clavering Road in Swallwell, appeared admirably suitable. At Consett a site was selected at Delves Lane.

Forty years before Bishop Auckland Fire Station acquired rescue boats, the Home Office allocated to the brigade a vehicle that carried three of these inflatable bikini rafts. They were powered by one of the vehicles, lightweight portable pumps.

The saga of the retained call-out sirens reared its ugly head again, this time in the Seaham district when a resident complained 'most strongly' against the use of the siren at Seaham Fire Station, particularly in the late evening. After due examination of the facts it was determined that in the previous twelve months the siren had only been sounded on twenty occasions, eleven of them between 7 a.m. and 6 p.m. and on six occasions between 10 p.m. and 11 p.m. Between 11 p.m. and 7 a.m. the sounding of the siren was expressly forbidden. During these times call bells in houses were used to alert the on-call firemen. Unfortunately, in the absence of suitable alternatives the siren was to stay. Other alternatives were looked at and one company did offer a system whereby the rise and fall of the siren could be blocked out and only the constant high-pitched noise heard but the sirens in the county were not suitable for such an adaptation. It is just as well the aggrieved Seaham resident did not live in Wheatley Hill as there were two sirens in this town, one at the fire station and one at the colliery where most of the firemen were employed.

New appliances continued to be delivered and in 1957 further Bedford-Miles water tenders were delivered and new vehicles ordered for delivery the next year were: another three Carmichael-bodied Karrier water tenders, one Bedford-Miles dual-purpose appliance, one turntable ladder to replace the Merryweather appliance at Stockton and an Austin Gypsy four-wheel-drive utility vehicle. Not all vehicles were equipped with radio when the scheme was first implemented – the equipment being rented from the Home Office – but gradually, as funding became available, the number of radio-equipped vehicles increased. Appliances at Langley Park,

The first new fire station at Spennymoor, built in 1958 at Queen Street, had an existence of just over twelve years, the site being cleared during redevelopment of the town centre.

Washington and Wheatley Hill were radio equipped in 1956 and the following year, in view of the wide areas covered, the second turn out appliances at Hebburn and Stockton were also equipped with radio. The new turntable ladder was delivered in the summer of 1958 and assigned to Stockton replacing the old open cab Exeter appliance which was sold to vehicle dismantlers at Benton, Newcastle. The new 160bhp Rolls-Royce petrol-engine turntable ladder, complete with built-in amidships mounted pump was based on a Dennis F27 chassis fitted with a 100ft ladder supplied by the German firm of Carl Metz. It was the first of the type in the country although Metz ladders mounted on Leyland chassis had been prevalent in the United Kingdom before the war and post-war; Dennis had marketed the ladders on earlier F14, F17 and F21 chassis before the F27 chassis that Durham adopted was developed. There were four principal European manufacturers of this type of ladder, Merryweather in London, Magirus and Metz in Germany and Geesink in Holland. Durham's choice of chassis for the new turntable ladder centred on two makes of vehicle, Bedford or Dennis. The quote for the Bedford was the lowest tender but on account of a greater horse power the second lowest tender from Guildford-based Dennis was accepted.

The new headquarters building at Framwellgate Moor was occupied in July 1957 and formally opened on 30 October. This was the first part of the complex; other buildings still to be erected were the brigade control facility, fire station, workshops and training school and another six years would pass before the whole site was completed to the original plans. Spennymoor's new fire station was occupied in July and also officially opened in October.

The first ten years of the history and development of the county fire authority in Durham had proved to be an interesting period for all members of the brigade, especially in the

The first stage of the new headquarters at Framwellgate Moor was completed in 1956 and comprised the administration block and the control room followed by the appliance room that was situated to the right of this structure.

An interior view of the new control room at Framwellgate Moor showing the disposition boards where the availability of all appliances and officers could be recorded.

All recruit firemen who attended the brigade's training school at Felling, and later Framwellgate Moor, were photographed at the end of the course. This 1958 course of recruit firemen at Felling are balanced on Billingham's Dennis Big 6 motor pump.

formative years when new officers had to be appointed, existing staff had to be transferred and the sometimes unsuitable premises that had been adopted as fire stations had to remain in use owing to Government spending constraints. Post-war restrictions on local authority building programs prevented the pace of modernisation progressing as quickly as would have been liked but considering this, many developments had taken place. The new headquarters had been erected, many sites for new fire stations had been secured and many of the wartime and pre-war fire engines had been replaced by modern counterparts. More years passed, however, before the entire renewal programme would be completed.

CHAPTER 2

NEW PREMISES

During the preceding financial year, 1 April 1957 to 31 March 1958, the tenth year of the countywide fire authorities existence, a total of 3,047 calls were dealt with of which 853 were actual fires, 785 involved chimneys, and malicious false alarms totalled seventy-eight. Chimney fires had shown an increase in over 50 per cent since the preceding twelve months.

At the beginning of 1958 the chief fire officer formulated the building plan for the next six years. This plan proposed the following:

1959–60

Aycliffe	Erection of a one-bay fire station, to be day-manned.
Crook	Erection of a one-bay retained fire station.
Durham	Erection of fire station, completion of drill yard and tower, stores and workshops.
Consett	Provision of engine house.

1960–61

Durham.	Completion of second phase of fire station.
Dunston	Erection of a new three-bay whole-time fire station.
Peterlee	Completion of phase two.

1960–61

Dunston	Completion of a new fire station.
Bishop Auckland	Completion of fire station.
Stockton	Erection of a new six-bay fire station.

1962–63

Stockton	Completion.
Hebburn	Erection of a new five-bay fire station.
Washington	Extension of a one-bay retained fire station.

1963–64

Hebburn	Completion.
Birtley	Erection of a two-bay fire station.
Hartlepool	Erection of a two-bay fire station.
Training School	Transfer from Felling to Durham.

1964–65

Completion of new training school.

Two new emergency tenders were ordered to replace the former wartime Fordson appliances. Billingham received the first one, pictured here next to its predecessor that operated thereafter as a foam tender. A similar pair operated at Hebburn.

New appliances on order included a new emergency tender to replace the converted war-time Fordson at Billingham. The chassis chosen was Bedford and Miles Engineering was appointed as the bodybuilder. There was less than £1 difference between the costs of the two lowest tenders, the other contender being Hampshire Car Bodies. Faced with a difficult decision, Miles Engineering was awarded the contract on the basis that the cost of collecting the vehicle was cheaper from Alfred Miles' premises at Cheltenham than it was from Hampshire Car Bodies Works near Southampton. The appliance was assigned to Billingham and was followed by a similar example for Hebburn. The receipt of these new vehicles displaced two former converted wartime Fordson vehicles, which were not disposed of but refitted as foam tenders, based at their original stations.

Fencehouses Fire Station, the opening of which saw the closure of the temporary fire stations at Houghton-le-Spring and Chester-le-Street, was formally opened by the chairman of the Fire Brigades Committee in November 1958. It was the first complete fire station to be built in the county, others before it being built in stages. The site for a new Birtley Fire Station was secured at the top of Edwards Road, just of Newcastle Road. The distance of the new fire station at Fencehouses meant that the establishment of a fire station at Birtley was secure for the foreseeable future. A site for Crook's new fire station was secured and at Chopwell the appliance was relocated to Messrs Maddisons & Haley's premises, opposite the fire station, whilst the station underwent alterations to enable a full-sized water tender to be housed within. Having evaluated two electric sirens fitted to appliances at Hebburn and Stockton and considering them to be more effective than bells, all appliances in the brigade were fitted with these devices. For many years afterwards the citizens of Durham County were privy to hearing the slow mournful wails

Fencehouses Fire Station, opened in October 1958, was the first completely new station in the County of Durham. Although the new stations at Bishop Auckland and Peterlee were operating they were built in two stages and were not completed until several years later.

of Francis's 'long rolling sirens'. Similar devices were also fitted to appliances at West Hartlepool and Middlesbrough but north of Durham, apart from one appliance in Sunderland, the fire bells remained the warning system of choice until the continental two-tone horns appeared in the mid-1960s. This was not the end of the traditional bells on Durham appliances though, as they were still kept as a secondary warning device should the sirens become defective.

Newcastle & Gateshead Joint Fire Service's fireboat, to which Durham contributed one third of the operating costs, was declared obsolete and withdrawn on the last day of November and the river fire station at Wincomblee, Walker, closed down. There was, however, a fireboat operated by the county borough of South Shields Fire Brigade to which the county also contributed and this now provided cover to the areas on the banks of the river Tyne at Hebburn, Jarrow, Bill Quay, Pelaw and further west at Dunston. The brigade also continued to share the operating costs of Middlesbrough's fireboat, covering the Tees's towns of Billingham, Stockton and Haverton Hill.

More wartime appliances were sold this year, together with twenty-six trailer pumps now declared obsolete with the continual introduction of new appliances fitted with lightweight pumps. There were still some pre-war Urban District Council appliances being used but one disposed of was former Stockton-on-Tees's Dennis New World appliance that worked out of Birtley in the post-war years. This appliance was involved in an accident on Christmas Eve 1958 and, with due consideration to the extensive damage sustained and the age of the appliance, it was declared a write-off and handed over to the insurers.

Recruiting for the AFS was still as slow as ever despite several big exercises being held at regular intervals. Aykley Heads was the venue for a water relay exercise in September, and in the following month a similar exercise using the bikini unit occurred at Monkton Coke Works.

During 1958 Chopwell Fire Station was rebuilt in order to accommodate a full-sized water tender. Here, the station is seen in its original state where the garage could only accommodate an old wartime towing vehicle.

In February 1959, eighty personnel with six green goddesses and hose lorry, pipe lorry, control unit and field cable unit attended an exercise at Hartlepool where it was supposed that the Municipal Buildings were on fire. Seventeen jets were put to work at this exercise through two water relays from the sea and river. The total of AFS personnel at the time was 225 men and fifty-two women. The number of females having reduced by over 50 per cent since the previous year and was reduced further to thirty-eight during the next twelve months. It appeared that the recruiting campaigns at which much effort was expended were merely topping up the existing staffing levels rather than swelling them and certainly in the case of the firewomen, there appeared little to motivate them to remain with the organisation.

Early 1959 saw some fairly heavy fire activity compared to the relatively quiet previous year. An eight-pump fire occurred at ICI Billingham's works in February when fifty tons of phenol spirit caught alight, and six pumps were required at a fire at Woolworths, Consett, the previous day. In March the three-storey Grey College, under construction in Durham city centre, suffered severe damage and fifteen pumps were assigned to attend. On 7 April ICI Billingham suffered another serious fire in the site's ammonia plant to which twenty pumps responded making this the county's biggest fire to date. On 21 April seven pumps attended a fire at the oil gasification plant at ICI Billingham and, as if this were not enough, a fire at the dri-kold plant at ICI Billingham took the effort of crews from ten pumps before it was contained. It can be seen that the petro-chemical works bounding the banks of the river Tees was a significant fire risk and was the scene of many major fires, despite the protection offered by the site's own fire brigade.

A graphic example of the adaptations undertaken during the brigade's early fire station replacement programme. Here the same fire station is pictured after the garage was extended to accommodate one of the new water tenders introduced into the service. The louvered box on the roof housed the call-out siren.

Over the years the fire brigade, by nature of the variety of work undertaken, received many commendations and letters of gratitude which are richly deserved but, like any organisation, they are not divorced from the odd person who appears dissatisfied. Occasionally, complaints are registered that take a considerable amount of time to investigate. One such complaint, received in April 1959, concerned an incident where a number of children were soaked by fire hoses whilst a grass fire was in progress at Esh Winning Wood. All members of the fire brigade that attended the incident emphatically denied directing water on to the children but agreed that during the course of the fire-fighting operations, spray was carried over a large area by the wind. Two police officers present confirmed that it had been difficult to contain the large number of children present who ignored orders to keep out of the way. Any wetting that occurred was accidental and 'would not have happened if they had done as told', said the police officers.

There had been a big increase in the number of calls attended by the brigade in 1959, notably in the small fires category. Of 3,409 small fires attended in a three-month period between 20 June and 19 September, 2,504 were calls to grass fires. On 19 November, a fire at Dans Castle School, Tow Law, needed a total of ten pumps before it was brought under control and at Dunston a fire at the British Paints factory was attended to by seven pumps. Animals were still getting themselves in precarious predicaments and, in April 1960, Sub-Officer R. James from Durham and Fireman O.W. Temple from Fencehouses both received the Certificate of Merit from the RSPCA for the rescue of a cat from the river Wear in November. Other Certificates of Merit had been awarded to Station Officer W. Tozer and Bishop Auckland Fire Station for the rescue of a cow from a well

at Marwood, Barnard Castle, in January 1958 and to Divisional Officer J. Clazey and Crook Fire Station for their rescue of a dog from Rogeley Quarry, Frosterley, in February. The rescue of a bullock in June 1960 saw the personnel of Barnard Castle Fire Station awarded the Certificate by Merit of the RSPCA.

In March 1960 the training school at Felling completed its forty-eighth recruits course at which Fireman J.L. Cairns from Durham was awarded the presentation silver axe. In April some employers of the British Transport Commission purposely set fire to a hut adjoining the railway at Tow Law, owing to its dangerous condition and because children were in the habit of playing in or around it. Because of its condition it was decided to have the hut demolished by fire on account of it being too dangerous to pull down. A passing motorist, however, called the fire brigade resulting in the attendance of an appliance from Crook which had to cross several fields belonging to Pitt House Farm to gain access and undo the work of the Transport Commission. On the way back the appliance became bogged down in one of the fields and had to be extricated by the brigade's breakdown lorry. This resulted in a claim being submitted from the landowner for damages to the crop and for valuation fees. The county council, on behalf of the fire brigade, settled for a reduced fee of ten pounds for the crop and two guineas for the valuation fees. Efforts were made to have the British Transport Commission make an ex-gratia payment to cover the farmer's loss without success. The costs were not recovered, as the commission contended that there was no need for the fire brigade to be called, as the fire was perfectly safe. In reply the county council stated that if the employers had remained on scene instead of leaving the burning hut unattended the fire brigade would not have been called out.

The wrangling over fire cover between the two Hartlepools, ongoing since 1953, still continued without agreement being reached, but the two brigades continued to provide a

Right: John Clark was a silver axe winner in 1961 and went on to have a distinguished career of over thirty years, retiring at the rank of senior divisional officer.

Opposite: Stanhope operated this wartime Fordson water tender with a pair of Sigmund pumps, one mounted on a trailer. Although quite rudimentary in design, these appliances were the forerunner of today's modern water tender. Sigmund pumps were of Czechoslovakian design, built under licence at Team Valley, Gateshead.

satisfactory service to their respective rate payers. A frequent special service call dealt with by the Hartlepool retained crews was to wash drifted sand from the lifeboat slipway at Middleton, Hartlepool. The men worked without payment and the fire brigade charitably waived all charges for these calls except the actual cost of petrol and oil used during the exercise.

In May the chrome ore works at Urlay Nook suffered a fire in the site's chrome oxide and tin plant at which ten pumps responded, and five days later another ten pumps were called to a warehouse in Stockton High Street. There were several heath and farm fires that required five or more pumps, such as Knitsley Fell in April where a half square mile of heathland was alight and Deeps Wood, Townsfield, the following day where 5 acres of fir trees, heather and bracken had ignited. In September a haystack fire at Stow House Farm, Cornsay Village, needed the attendance of six pumps before sufficient water could be brought to bear on a four-bay Dutch barn containing 140 tons of hay.

More appliances were disposed of that year including the former Billingham Urban District Council's pre-war Dennis Big six-pump escape which went to a buyer in Newcastle.

Recruits Course No.51 commenced in January 1961 and another Durham fireman, John A. Clark proudly won the coveted presentation silver axe. This was the start of a fulfilling career, as he remained in the service for thirty-three years, retiring in 1994 at the rank of divisional officer and having just been awarded the Queens Fire Service Medal. The new Consett Fire Station at Delves Lane was ready for use by the end of February and formally opened on 26 March and at last, a fire station at Aycliffe was formally opened on 1 November. Crook's new fire station became operational during the same month, equipped with one appliance and ten newly trained retained firemen.

Wheatley Hill firemen were victors again in the national quiz competition, reaching the finals after gaining a win at the semi-finals at Leeds in March when they gained forty-one and a half marks out of a possible forty-five, beating the next highest team from Lancashire by ten points.

In 1961 several Hampshire Car Bodies water tenders on Bedford chassis were delivered but this was the only one equipped to carry a wheeled escape. It served all of its life at Seaham and forms a backdrop to early examples of walkie-talkie radios.

At the finals, held in April at the Fire Service College, Dorking, Surrey, the four-man team, captained by Station Officer Poulson, was victorious and on return the team was quite deservedly commended by the chairman of the Fire Brigades' Committee.

In March 1961 Burnhope Miners' Hall became a casualty to fire and ten days later a Clothing Factory at Dean Bank, Ferryhill, and two adjacent Nissen-type huts saw a total of fifteen pumps mobilised. Sacriston Institute was severely damaged by fire on 15 December and on the 20th the District Mobilising Scheme was initiated again, with twelve Durham appliances responding to a major fire at Luxdon Laundry in the borough of Sunderland. 10,000 bundles of laundry comprising about 100,000 articles were destroyed in this blaze. Once again Sunderland Fire Brigade's chief fire officer, Leslie Allinson, was full of praise for the supporting appliance crews from South Shields, Seaham, Durham, Felling, Hebburn, Washington, and Fencehouses. 'The Durham County Chief, Mr. C.V. Hall is really a good neighbour,' said Mr Allinson. 'He not only sent more pumps than we asked for but also a canteen van which was more than welcome on such a cold night.'

An old open-topped Dennis Braidwood pump escape that served in London during the war and was transferred to Durham in 1948 for use at the brigade training school was sold in October 1961 and disappeared for many years before reappearing in the late 1990s in South Wales, fully restored. Hebburn's Dennis F12 dual-purpose appliance, operational there since 1951, underwent a conversion where the small eighty-gallon water tank was replaced by a more functional tank of 300-gallon capacity. By the end of 1961 every fire station was equipped with

The former Billingham Urban District Council Dennis Big six-pump escape was sold in 1961 having given just over twenty years of service. In the years leading up to its disposal it was based at the training school at Felling.

new post-war pumping appliances. It had taken thirteen years to achieve this but there were still some pre-war appliances on the fleet strength, notably at the training school, which continued to use these types of appliances right up until the 1970s. They often attended major fires with recruits from the training school in order to give them some early fire-fighting or fire ground experience. Some wartime conversions were also still in service such as the canteen van and control unit at Durham and the foam tenders at Billingham and Hebburn.

The firemen's working week, previously reduced down to fifty-six hours, was reduced even further when it was recommended, in 1961, that the working week be further reduced to one of forty-eight hours. Introduced in 1962, this reduction in hours meant an increase to the establishment of forty-eight men, comprising thirty-six leading firemen and twelve firemen.

Tenders were submitted for the construction of a new fire station at Hartlepool and the opening of Swallwell Fire Station saw the closure of the station at Dunston, although the living accommodation was retained for housing the recruits from the training school at Felling. A disused AFS garage at Dunston was transferred to Washington and the control unit housed therein transferred to Seaham. The new Consett Fire Station, occupied by March, was formally opened on 26 May and the lease for the old premises at Park Avenue terminated.

The attendance of the fire brigade at road accidents has formed a steadily increasing workload for firefighters. In 1961 Durham County Fire Brigade replaced their wartime breakdown lorry with this comprehensively equipped four-wheel-drive Bedford appliance.

A site was also secured for the new Hebburn Fire Station at Victoria Road opposite Mill Lane. The second stage of Peterlee and Bishop Auckland stations, delayed by extremes of weather, were both nearing completion and the new fire stations at Crook and Newton Aycliffe were opened. Large fires during 1962 were recorded at the Old Nursery School, New Brancepeth, in February (seven pumps), West Cornforth Cooperative Stores in May (ten pumps), Helmington Grange Farm, Crook (ten pumps) in August and St Chad's College, Durham (five pumps) in November. An emergency special service call in November saw Peterlee crews respond in severe weather conditions to a road accident on the Horden to Blackhall road. Two private cars and a tanker laden with 14 tons of sulphuric acid had collided. The fire brigade assisted with the rescue operations and, at the request of the police, washed away sulphuric acid leaking from the overturned tanker. This type of incident, although not infrequent, was rarely attended by the fire brigade but in years to come road accidents became an increasing feature of the workload of the fire service. Fire has little respect for those not fully aware of its demonic properties and this was no less demonstrated in December, on the last hour of Christmas Day, when three little sisters tragically lost their lives in a fire that destroyed their wooden bungalow at Finchale Caravan Park. The children's mother managed to escape the fire with her seventeen-month-old daughter but despite heroic attempts by others on the site the intensity of the fire was such that sadly the young girls could not be saved.

Since the formation of the brigade in 1948 the senior officer establishment had been reasonably consistent but in May 1962 it was announced that the assistant chief fire officer, Charles Tozer, would be retiring in November upon reaching the age of sixty. He had been in the post since the formation

Dunston Fire Station on Dunston Road, pictured in 1949 when it was equipped, in common with most of the county's fire stations, by wartime standard fire engines. It closed in 1962 when the new Swallwell Fire Station opened.

of the brigade in 1948 and was awarded the King's Police and Fire Service Medal in 1952 for distinguished service. The Tozer name was carried on by son William who, after a brief spell with the Auxiliary Fire Service, joined the brigade proper in 1948 as a retained fireman at Dunston. Since that time he had progressively risen through the ranks and at the time of his father's retirement he had attained the rank of divisional officer. It became necessary to advertise the impending assistant chief fire officer vacancy and of the six officers shortlisted, including two internal applicants, Divisional Officer J.W. (Jimmy) Smith was appointed to the post. Mr Smith's fire service career started in 1937 when he enrolled in the old Chester-le-Street Urban District Council Fire Brigade as fireman/engineer. By 1941 he was chief fire officer of the brigade. During the reign of the National Fire Service he served in various positions as company officer and column officer, and on the formation of the new county fire authority he transferred over at the rank of assistant divisional officer. The divisional officer's vacant post was filled by an applicant from West Bromwich, Mr D.J. Bruce. The following year, following a period of hospitalisation, the chief fire officer also announced his intention to retire from the post he had held for the last fifteen years. Six applicants and two reserves were shortlisted for this impending vacancy and J.W. Smith, only recently appointed as the assistant chief fire officer, secured the post. William Hagan was then appointed as the new assistant chief fire officer. This officer's career commenced in 1937 as a part-time fireman in the Auxiliary Fire Service at South Shields and during the reign of the NFS he served as section leader, becoming a regional staff instructor in 1947 before being promoted to company officer two years later. On denationalisation he was appointed station officer with the Durham County Fire Brigade at Chester-le-Street, later rising to the ranks of assistant divisional officer and divisional officer at Hebburn.

In 1962, J.W. Smith became the second person to hold the post of chief fire officer of Durham County Fire Brigade, but his tenure was only short, he retired in 1967.

Problems occurred with the Middlesbrough fireboat in 1962 when the need to replace the engines of the boat was identified. At a cost of £25,000 Durham County Fire Brigade did not see this as an economical proposition to contribute to. Instead, joint arrangements were made with the North Riding of Yorkshire Fire Brigade for the hire of launches from Smiths Dock Co., Grangetown, in the event that water-borne craft was needed to fight fires in the Durham districts that bordered the river Tees. In the not too distant future the particular risks of fire-fighting in the heavily industrialised areas of the river Tees would cease to be the responsibility of Durham County Fire Brigade. The Hartlepool saga was resurrected again this year culminating in an inquiry at County Hall, Durham, at which Mr A.V. Thomas GM from Her Majesty's Inspectorate of Fire Services attended as an assessor. If not resolved this time, it would certainly be resolved in the not too distant future but not in a way that was predicted at this time. The borough's new two-bay retained fire station at Durham Street on the Headland was nearing completion and opened for business during the week leading up to Christmas.

Two new Bedford appliances arrived that year, both Carmichael-bodied water tenders that were assigned to Hebburn and Stockton and were the only examples of this type of appliance to be purchased by the authority. No more appliances from Alfred Miles were delivered as the company was incorporated into the Dennis Group around this time. In May the brigade's second new turntable ladder arrived. Based on a similar Dennis F27 chassis as Stockton's, this vehicle, supplied by David Haydon & Sons, had ladder equipment manufactured by the German firm of Magirus as opposed to a Metz ladder of the previous turntable appliance. The differences were fairly obvious – the Metz ladder was characterised by the square sections of the ladder and the large chain-driven mechanisms that elevated it. The new vehicle was assigned to Durham, displacing the old wartime Austin machine which was sold to Rentokil Laboratories, Glasgow.

The work of the fire service is generally publicised by its activities within the public domain, often in tragic circumstances, but there is another equally important activity of the organisation, that of fire prevention, and the education of the public with the basic objective of preventing fires before they occur. Under the Durham County Council Act, which received Royal Assent in July 1963, Durham County Fire Brigade was the first fire authority in the country to have powers to inspect premises used by unlicensed clubs for entertainment, dancing or playing games. Among other things the Act empowered district councils to require the owners or occupiers of such premises to provide and maintain satisfactory means of entry and exit, passageways and gangways and the provision of adequate fire-fighting equipment and permit the fire authority to prescribe standard signs for buildings where substances likely to create fire-fighting hazards were stored. In October of the following year a scheme was introduced whereby fire service personnel arranged, with the consent of householders, visits to residential properties for the purpose of giving advice on precautions against fire. Almost 6,000 houses were visited, during which the commonest faults noted were with items of electrical equipment and the general lack of fireguards. It is commendable to note that no occupier refused the offer of this service.

Durham still burned. In April 1964 eight pumps attended a fire at the Malleable Works, Stockton, and in June eight pumps were required at Framwellgate Moor Secondary Modern School. A similar number of pumps attended a fire at St Patrick's Church, Dipton, in June and five pumps were required at fires at the Tivoli Picture House, Southmoor, in July and Dunston Flour Mills in Swallwells area in August. This period had been one of the busiest for the brigade with 110 calls received in a single day. In all, 6,335 calls were dealt with, 395 of them being of malicious origin. Malicious false alarms were being received at the rate of over one per day and continued to plague not only Durham County Fire Brigade but the country as a whole.

The arrangements that existed with Middlesbrough Fire Brigade regarding the Tees fireboat were annulled in 1962 and arrangements made instead with Smiths Dock Co. in the event of a boat being needed for fire-fighting purposes. The Middlesbrough boat is pictured just abeam of its moorings near the Transporter Bridge.

Durham's second new Turntable ladder featured equipment by Magirus and is pictured on the forecourt at Framwellgate Moor shortly after delivery. Note that the appliance has its own built-in pump.

The Fire Bug Will Get You If You Don't Watch Out! This dragon, mounted on the brigade's new lorry in 1964, was rigged up to exhale smoke as part of the season's fire prevention campaign.

In order to stimulate recruitment to the AFS and provide a suitable training area, a camp was established at Hamsterley Forest where AFS crews from Durham and surrounding brigades could attend weekend courses. A similar camp had previously been established in Northumberland's Kielder Forest for use by the AFS personnel of Northumberland County Fire Brigade. Hamsterley Forest became the regular training ground for the county's AFS personnel with frequent weekend training exercises held there under the name Exercise 'Hard Tack' or Exercise 'Dig to Live', where the crews camped on the appliances and fed themselves from field kitchens. Hutted accommodation for forty personnel was erected at Hamsterley. As the strength of the AFS increased so too did the number of green appliances allocated by the Home Office until the inventory included twelve green goddess emergency pumps, thirteen other vehicles, nine motorcycles and twenty-one light portable pumps. Other regular weekend exercises were held at Washington Hall, Chorley in Lancashire and, in July 1961, ninety AFS personnel with seventy appliances attended 'Exercise Tidereach' at South Shields. Most fire stations had additional garage accommodation erected to house the additional vehicles and in some cases the complex act of dismantling garages at one station and re-erecting them at another was undertaken. These transfers were not always successful though. In 1963 plans to transfer a garage from Crook to Consett were thwarted when the building, in the process of re-erection at Consett, was completely demolished by gale-force winds, rendering it completely beyond repair. Instead a garage at Hebburn was dismantled and transferred to Consett.

Following a scheme introduced to the London Fire Brigade in January 1964, Durham County Fire Brigade introduced its own Junior Fireman Scheme, a new recruitment scheme for the appointment of junior firemen in order to produce more recruits of good standards.

Hamsterley Forest during one of the many weekend 'Dig to Live' or 'Hard Tack' exercises. Here the crew of an AFS canteen van set up ready to feed the mouths of the hungry volunteers. (G. and A. Pringle)

The scheme provided for the enrolment of cadet firemen at the age of sixteen who would undertake two years' college, fire service training and education, physical fitness training and the chance to attend outward bound courses at the end of which, following the standard recruits course, they would become professional firemen.

In March 1965 a team from Wheatley Hill were once again high achievers in the National Quiz Competition and won the semi-finals at Wigan, qualifying the team for the finals at the Fire Service College, Dorking, in April. The new Stockton Fire Station at Norton was formally opened in July 1965 by the Home Office inspector, W.E. Norwood, and the old stations at Billingham and Stockton closed down with appliances and staff from both relocated to Norton. The new six-bay station with two additional garages in the rear yard for AFS vehicles and a two-storey breathing apparatus gallery in the drill yard was built at a cost of £84,000. Something taken for granted now but a novel feature in this particular era was the electrically operated appliance room doors that could be operated from the watchroom or the appliance room. Hebburn also got its new fire station at the end of July, built on similar lines to the Stockton one but with only a five-bay appliance room. The opening of the new Hebburn Fire Station saw the closure of the old stations at Hedgeley Road, Hebburn, and Carlisle Street, Felling; the training school having moved to Framwellgate Moor in 1963. The establishment at Hebburn was increased by the addition of one water tender from Felling, to be manned on a part-time basis by retained crews. However, after canvassing every house within 400 yards of the new station in an endeavour to recruit twelve part-timers, not one person was enrolled. Until the matter was resolved the pump was manned on a whole-time basis.

Many females enrolled in the AFS where they excelled, in communications duties especially. Durham's control unit is seen at an exercise at Tyne Dock, South Shields, together with some of the control room staff. Even the motorcycle despatch rider is female.

These AFS garages were portable and moved from station to station as required. This Billingham garage accommodates one of the new 'atomic' green goddess fire engines, introduced in 1954, some of which still existed in Government stores in 2006.

Two of these Carmichael-bodied water tenders were delivered in 1964, one for Hebburn and the other for Stockton. Hebburn's example is pictured at a fire at Marconi's, Bill Quay, in the late 1960s. Apart from the river Tyne, nothing exists here now, neither the appliances nor the shipyards behind.

It had taken many years to achieve but the old, unsuitable fire stations were gradually being replaced as funding permitted. Plans were revealed for the establishment of a new day manning station at Eaglescliffe, together with ten houses for the firemen, to be financed in the 1968–69 budget. A major improvement for the brigade's wireless communication system occurred in 1965 when the brigade was allocated its own wireless scheme and radio frequency, no longer having to share the same scheme and frequency as the police. It was at this time that the brigade control adopted the 'M2LF' call sign and all the vehicle call signs were numbered according to the station's location, prefixed by the word 'Foxtrot'. Darlington and Hartlepool fire brigades also separated from the police scheme and shared the new frequency with the county fire brigade, using the 'talk through' facility.

Several large fires occurred this year. Young's Motors, Chester-le-Street, required an attendance of ten pumps in March and the ICI Works at Billingham was the scene of several serious fires. On 10 April, five pumps were called to a fire at the ICI Oil Works and on 13 May ten pumps attended the ammonia plant. Eight days later a fire at the synthesis plant at ICI was dealt with by the crews from five pumps and in June crews were back at the oil works for a fire that required six pumps. There were four more five-pump incidents at the plant, one in each of June and September and two in October. As the above illustrates, the complexities and risks inherent in the petro-chemical plants at Billingham were the source of frequent attendances by the fire brigade. Within a few years these risks would cease to be a problem for the county fire brigade but not because of good housekeeping at the plant. On the last day of January 1966 ten pumps were required for a fire at ICI's North Tees works.

The opening of a new fire station at Norton saw the closure of Stockton's old fire station in West Row, pictured here in 1948 with the town's two pre-war appliances, a Leyland and Dennis parked on the ramp.

There were still some old wartime appliances in service in the county in 1966, and three pre-war appliances still remained on the inventory, but the number of wartime appliances was reduced by two when the old Fordson foam tenders at Stockton and Hebburn were sold together with the two Leyland Comets purchased in 1950. The foam tenders were replaced by redundant Commer-Miles water tenders, rebuilt and converted by brigade workshop staff into foam tenders. The county's Auxiliary Fire Service was still highly active and, in September, at the invitation of the Greater London Council, the chairman of the Fire Brigade's Committee and the chief fire officer together with a contingent of eight AFS appliances and twenty-two personnel made the long journey to London to participate in the largest exercise ever to be held in the United Kingdom. Exercise 'Tercentenary' centred at the 'Royal' group of docks in London was organised to commemorate the 300th anniversary of the Great Fire of London.

Peterlee's crews had a busy time in April when ten pumps were required at a fire at McGregor's wallpaper factory. In June a fire at the Rex Cinema, Consett, was extinguished by crews from eight pumps and, in August, five pumps were back at ICI's synthesis plant in Billingham. September saw crews from Billingham ordering reinforcements at fires at ICI Oil Works (twelve pumps) and a transformer station fire at Stockton, (eleven pumps). In the extreme north of the county eight pumps attended a fire at Peartree Garage, Felling Road in the Hebburn area. There was no let-up for the Stockton crews – or for ICI – as in October eight pumps attended a fire at the site's aromatic plant and, two months later, the ammonia plant required an attendance of twelve pumps. As was always the case the valiant crews worked long and hard to prevent the fires from spreading and involving greater areas of the plant and yet, despite the precautions and

An early view of Billingham Fire Station, shown just after the formation of the county fire brigade. Awaiting the next call are an Austin towing vehicle and a pre-war Dennis motor pump. This station also closed on the opening of a new fire station at Norton.

When the new fire station at Hebburn opened, Felling's Bedford water tender and the watches that manned it transferred to the new station at Hebburn making it a three-pump station. The appliance on the far side is one of the Miles-bodied Dennis appliances, in use as a reserve. (Ian Moore)

fire prevention regulations of the time, fires did occasionally get out of control. On 16 January 1967 Stockton crews were mobilised once again to a fire call at ICI's North Tees works at Port Clarence. Occurring just before 4 p.m., five appliances from Stockton were turned out to a fire in No.2 crude unit at North Tees Refinery and, whilst en route to the site, flames reaching to a height of 300ft and visible from 10 miles away made it fairly obvious to the responding crews that a major fire was in progress. A message was immediately transmitted back to brigade control advising them of the situation and requesting a total of ten pumps to be mobilised to the incident. On arrival a severe fire was in progress in a 100ft fractioning column. Site workers in the vicinity were in the process of being evacuated and at least one person was reported unaccounted for. Six cooling jets were immediately brought to bear on surrounding structures supplementing four jets already in use by the site's works fire brigade. A 'Major Fire' message was sent by the station officer together with a request for extra foam supplies and the super foam monitor. On the arrival of the chief fire officer a water relay had already been established from the river Tees and further ground monitors were ordered to cool the structural steel work around the column in an attempt to prevent the spread of fire and collapse; the tower already inclining to a dangerous degree. As the fire progressed it was confirmed that three site workers were unaccounted for but searches for the missing men were hampered by the intensity of the fire. As 5 p.m. approached sixteen water jets were in operation and, shortly after, the fire was contained but continued to burn for some time owing to a fractured pipeline from an overhead oil storage tank. By midnight the monitors were reduced to eight but it was not until the next evening that the fire was finally declared under control with three crews remaining on site cooling down the affected areas in order to prevent re-ignition. Owing to the complexity of the area involved and the dangers of re-ignition, it was not until six days after the fire started that a third missing man was finally located. In all, three site workers lost their lives. A total of twenty-six pumps were mobilised to the fire making this incident the biggest in the county, an accolade that, at this time, has fortunately not since been exceeded. Durham County Fire Brigade's appliances travelled from as far away as Hebburn and Fencehouses and, under the district mobilising arrangements, outside assistance was received from the North Riding of Yorkshire's fire brigades at Grangetown, Redcar and Thornaby, together with one appliance each from Darlington, Middlesbrough and West Hartlepool county boroughs.

Every year the fire brigade received many letters of thanks for the humane and professional services rendered and one such letter, from the Refinery Site manager at ICI Ltd, reproduced in its entirety, is self explanatory:

I thank you once again for the way in which you and your officers and men tackled the shocking incident we had at North Tees on Monday, 16-1-1967. It is really amazing to me that you were able to mount such a fantastic effort in such a short time and the containment of what was a very difficult situation. The incident itself, especially as lives were lost, was tragic, but how much worse it could have been had the fire not been contained in a comparatively small area as it was. I do thank you once again and most sincerely I would ask you to convey the thanks of us all at North Tees to all officers and men who were called to the site.

Another letter, received from the general manager of neighbouring Phillips Imperial Petroleum Ltd, joint operator of the site, was just as praiseworthy of the fire brigade's efforts, especially the fact that the crews were more concerned with controlling the fire than with their own safety! This fire was, without any doubt, the biggest in the brigade's history and was fought, contained and extinguished only with great courage and tenacity from all the crews concerned.

A major fire at ICI's site at Billingham in January 1967 was the county's biggest fire to date. Flames engulf the 70ft-high distillation column during the height of the fire. (*Newcastle Chronicle & Journal*)

As far as large fires go, the remainder of 1967 was relatively quiet; eight pumps were needed at a fire at British Titan Works, Billingham, in August, six pumps at Stone Cellars Farm, Washington, and in December ten pumps, including one from Newcastle & Gateshead Joint Fire Service, were despatched to Blaydon Cooperative Society's premises at Chopwell which was well alight when the first crew arrived. Two firemen were transported to hospital suffering injuries at what was described as the worst fire in the local district for many years. Tins of produce, exploding like shells, hampered fire-fighting and so severe was the damage that the remaining walls had to be demolished. District mobilising, co-ordinated from the Durham County Fire Brigade control room, was initiated again that year when twenty pumps and three turntable ladders were required to fight a major fire at a cigarette component warehouse in South Shields Fire Brigade's area during March. Although the mobilising scheme had been instigated on several previous occasions, for Sunderland Fire Brigade this was the first time that South Shields Fire Brigade had reason to initiate it. Just over two years later South Shields Fire Brigade had to implement district mobilising again when fire destroyed a dry and frozen foods distribution warehouse on the Simonside Industrial Estate. Although not in Durham's area, two appliances from Hebburn Fire Station were turned out on the initial call whereupon it was evident that a major fire was in progress and a request for eight pumps to be mobilised was made whilst en route to the fire. In all twenty pumps, eight of them from Durham County, together with the canteen van, attended this fire. The number of fire calls attended to during the previous twelve months totalled 5,622, which included 3,089 actual fires, 1,115 chimney fires and 469 malicious false alarms. There were 666 fires involving gorse, grass and shrubbery and 1,880 fires in dwelling houses, a reduction from the previous year put down to the beneficial effects of inspections from the fire prevention officers who undertook visits to 3,819 homes for the purposes of giving advice on fire prevention in the home.

CHAPTER 3

REORGANISATIONS

The long-running problems regarding fire cover in the Hartlepools was resolved overnight when, on 1 April 1967, Durham County Council's Hartlepool Fire Station and its two pumps and twenty personnel were incorporated into the newly formed County Borough of Hartlepool Fire Brigade. No longer would there be a need for discussion regarding the responsibility of receipt of fire calls and joint attendances in each other's areas. Under Hartlepool ownership the former Durham station kept its part-time status and continues to do so, albeit following yet another re-organisation of local boundaries. Exactly one year later, further boundary changes occurred which saw the formation of the new County Borough of Teesside, incorporating Middlesbrough, part of North Riding of Yorkshire and the Stockton and Billingham areas of Durham County. This re-organisation saw Norton Fire Station, consistently the county's busiest, transferred out of the county of Durham and into Teesside taking with it five appliances and eighty personnel. The emergency tender was not part of the transfer agreement. Within twelve months the county of Durham had lost a heavily industrialised and populated area, the population in Durham now equating to approximately 825,000 and, in the not too distant future, more areas would be pared away reducing the population even further. At Seaham where the fire brigade covered its own area as well as the Ryhope area of Sunderland, served by the Ryhope telephone exchange, it was determined by the chief fire officer that the fire risk only marginally justified the protection provided by one whole-time and one retained appliance and advocated that consideration should be given to the station operating on a day-manned system. Authorisation for the building of ten new houses to accommodate the firemen was sought and, when completed, the new day-manning arrangements would result in an annual saving of more than half the cost of the existing manning arrangements. The Fire Brigades Union was vehemently against such a proposal on the basis that the new system would force members to undertake an extra 'one day's hours' of duty in excess of the original system.

Spennymoor's recently constructed new fire station was short-lived as the redevelopment of the town centre and the second stage of the construction of a shopping centre by Arndale Developments Ltd involved the relocation of the single-bay fire station from Queen Street to another site at Bessemer Park. These complications would not be too much of a problem for Chief Fire Officer Smith for, soon to reach the age of sixty, it was announced that it was his intention to retire in October 1967, after having commanded the brigade for just five years. Among the applicants for the impending vacancy two chief fire officers, one deputy chief fire officer, three assistant chief fire officers and one assistant fire master including the assistant chief fire officers of both Durham and Northumberland and the chief fire officer of South Shields were shortlisted. Mr Duncan James Park Walker, chief fire officer of South Shields, was the successful applicant second time around and commenced his tenure on 9 October 1967. He had previously applied for the last chief fire officer's vacancy at Durham but was not successful.

Hartlepool Headland Fire Station transferred to West Hartlepool Fire Brigade in April 1967 and with it went this Bedford Miles water tender, pictured just after the transfer. The only other appliance of this type in Durham operated from Washington. (I. Moore)

His patience paid off. Also in October that year, Assistant Chief Fire Officer Bill Hagan was hospitalised suffering from burns after falling into a naphthalene fire at Brancepeth Coke Works. This fire involved tanks of naphthalene in a corrugated-iron shed, the whole of which was destroyed despite the efforts of thirty men and six engines.

By the year's end the AFS had received a new Morris mini van, one BSA motorcycle for use by despatch riders and another green goddess, and twenty-one weekend courses had been held at Hamsterley Forest. The establishment figures at the time numbered 251 men and fifty-nine women members. These new additions to the fleet were short-lived, as at the same time the Government announced the shock decision of the disbanding of the Civil Defence Corps and the Auxiliary Fire Service effectively ending one of the most illustrious of organisations. Defence cuts and cuts in Government spending saw a majority vote in favour of the disbanding of the civil defence organisations and on 31 March 1968 the AFS ceased to be. All AFS vehicles were returned to Home Office stores for long-term storage or disposal by auction, marking the end of the green appliances not only in Durham but the rest of the country. Well almost, as they were to reappear in the future but not for a re-established AFS.

One of the first tasks of the new chief fire officer was a review of the county's fire cover and establishment which determined that, apart from the proposed new fire station at Eaglescliffe and the acquisition of an emergency tender for Durham, there had been no increase in fire-fighting appliances since the formation of the brigade in 1948. The chief fire officer declared at the Fire Brigade Committee meeting in July 1968:

Duncan J.P. Walker, chief fire officer of South Shields Fire Brigade, was appointed chief fire officer of Durham County Fire Brigade in October 1967 replacing J.W. Smith.

The illustrious Auxiliary Fire Service was disbanded at the end of March 1968 and all the appliances returned to Home Office stores. Mobile column and convoy exercises were regular features during the organisations existence as demonstrated by these Durham units. (Brett Clayton)

The future structure of the brigade must necessarily be determined by recent changes in the county boundaries, the continual closure of collieries and consequent dispersal of sources of retained manpower and the introduction of new industries and increasing fire risks.

Despite repeated attempts, the brigade had still not been able to recruit a suitable cadre of retained personnel to man the third pump at Hebburn Fire Station, so it was proposed that the temporary whole-time manning of the third pump be made permanent. At Washington, which was shortly to obtain 'Newtown' status and a new day-manned fire station in place of the current retained pump, the fact that the appliance covered parts of Felling and Boldon as well as the Washington area suggested that a review of the fire cover was needed here. In view of the scale of developments in the proposed new town it was decided that the retained appliance and personnel be kept on strength and continue to operate, together with the planned day-manned appliance. Other proposals included a second water tender escape appliance at Durham and the establishment of second pumps at Spennymoor, Stanhope, Sedgefield and Newton Aycliffe. More controversial was the suggestion to introduce day-manning at Consett, Stanley, Fencehouses and

Swallwell with the aim of having a smaller, highly trained and more highly paid service relative to the needs of the fire brigade area with systems that should be more economic in the use of manpower, consistent with the regular standards of cover. The proposals were accepted in principal and, apart from the day-manning alterations, most were carried out. Further amendments to the establishment were proposed for Peterlee Fire Station where, since 1954, the population had increased by 16,000 and industrial sites expanded to cover over 49 acres with 109 premises requiring an initial attendance of two pumps. In one eight-month period the retained appliance at Peterlee was not available on 533 occasions owing to difficulties in recruiting suitable part-time firemen to man it. In the previous ten years there had been a turnover of thirty men, none of them serving more than twelve months, with some of them serving for as little as four weeks. Compounded with this was the situation at neighbouring Wheatley Hill where the closure of the colliery at which many of the retained personnel were employed and the consequent inability of the remaining personnel to respond accordingly had resulted in the second appliance not being manned from 8.00 a.m. until 2.00 p.m. on most weekdays during the previous twelve months. The untenable situation and the lack of any foreseeable improvement was a precursor to the second appliance at Peterlee being manned by whole-time personnel and the termination of the remaining retained personnel. Despite the problems at Wheatley Hill, the station's quiz team still managed to gain first place in the 1969 Northern semi-finals of the competition for retained personnel, granting them a place in the national finals at the Fire Service College at Dorking in April.

Between 1964 and 1968 the brigade received eight of these HCB-Angus-bodied water tender and water tender escapes. This 1966 model was based at Framwellgate Moor, where all new appliances generally went before being handed down to other stations as newer appliances were delivered.

The rural firefighters of Sedgefield were turned out in the early morning hours of 15 May 1968 to a fire that was of such an extent that fifteen pumps were needed before it could be brought under control and it was only through the efforts of the firefighters that the fire was prevented from spreading to an oil-storage farm. The premises concerned, Berry Wiggins & Macoil, consisted of ranges of single-storey bitumen storage and distribution plant. En route to the incident a message was sent to brigade control requesting ten pumps and a foam tender to be despatched where, on arrival, it was found that a bitumen heater house was well alight and the fire was spreading to adjacent storages and garages. Major difficulties were experienced with inadequate water supplies and water had to be relayed from hydrants almost a mile away reinforced by supplies from a portable pump set into a stream. Within just one and a half hours the fire was brought under control.

The attendance of the fire brigade at road accidents was becoming an increasingly common occurrence and the construction of the A1M motorway through the county prompted the brigade to consider increasing the current number of emergency tenders, notably to cover the Washington and Birtley areas where the nearest emergency tender equipped with rescue equipment had to travel from Durham, Hebburn or Newcastle. One redundant water tender, equipped with compressed air-cutting equipment, 'Flexiforce' hydraulic rams, Minuteman resuscitator and miscellaneous tools, was duly converted for the purpose and assigned to Birtley, alternately manned with one of the water tenders. A second appliance was converted for similar duties at Ferryhill until additional accommodation was made available at Newton Aycliffe. In addition, twenty-one portable cutting tools for rescue purposes were placed on every first turn-out appliance in the brigade.

There were several major fires in the region during 1969, two of them in the county of Durham occurring within two weeks of each other. The first one occurred at Durham City's famous carpet factory, Hugh Mackays, underneath the New Elvet Bridge on 5 May. Factory personnel discovered the fire at just after 2 a.m., in a bin containing jute shuttles. Believing this to be the main seat of fire they attempted to extinguish it using a hose reel, but were eventually beaten back by smoke. At about 2.35 a.m. a Durham County retained fireman employed in another part of the factory was informed and, realising that breathing apparatus was required, he immediately told the foreman to call the fire brigade and evacuate the factory. On arrival of the appliances from Framwellgate Moor, the Wilton Shed was found to be heavily smoke-logged. Two firemen wearing breathing apparatus could not locate the seat of the fire and just after they left the building the fire exploded through the roof. Attempts to surround the building were thwarted due to its age and construction, and the fire spread rapidly along the north side, leapfrogging from one bay to another and endangering surrounding buildings. At 3.04 a.m. a total of ten pumps were ordered to the fire and forty minutes later the number was increased to fifteen. Three turntable ladders from Durham, Gateshead and Sunderland also attended. The fire was brought under control at 5.24 a.m. Damage was confined to the west bay of the Wilton Shed, however, despite the damage, production was unaffected in the Axminster Department and was able to recommence within a fortnight in the east bay of the Wilton Shed. This was the biggest fire ever to have occurred within the city of Durham and damage was estimated at over £500,000. Just two weeks later Fencehouses's crews were called out to the Arcade, in the main shopping thoroughfare of Chester-le-Street, where a furniture shop was reported to be on fire. Within minutes of staff leaving the shop at the end of the working day the whole arcade was well alight, with the fire spreading into a four-storey building above. At an early stage of the incident firefighters had to be withdrawn, as it was feared that a large area of the front wall of

An unusual view of Seaham's water tender escape as it draughts water from the river Wear during the Mackay's Carpet Factory fire. The wheeled escape has been removed and pitched to the New Elvet Bridge to allow access to both levels of the building.

the building might collapse. Thanks to the gallant efforts of the fire crews the fire was prevented from spreading to adjoining property, which included a Woolworths store and a large furniture shop. Fifteen pumps attended this fire together with two turntable ladders and additional specialist appliances. One major pump from Newcastle & Gateshead Fire Service attended, with the second turntable ladder coming from Sunderland Fire Brigade. The rapidly spreading fire engulfed the wheeled escape of Fencehouses's appliance causing enough damage to result in it being written off by the insurers. The total fire damage amounted to £250,000. Chester-le-Street was the scene of another tragedy some months earlier, in April, when a house fire at Albert Terrace took the lives of a mother and her four young children aged between eleven months and seven years of age. Occurring at 7 a.m., another sibling – aged six – was brought to safety by the father, both of whom survived the tragedy. In August twelve pumps were used at Reeds Crane Hire, Factory Road, Blaydon, where a plant hire depot and frozen food factory were destroyed in a fire believed to have been started by a spark from a welder's torch which ignited a 500-gallon tank of diesel oil. The three-storey building was totally destroyed. Neighbouring Smedley's Frozen Food factory and 40 tons of frozen food were destroyed and a firm of timber importers had its entire stock destroyed. Two firemen sustained injuries at the fire, one of them, from Newcastle & Gateshead Joint Fire Service, requiring removal to hospital. In October, five pumps attended a fire at Clayton Davies Shipbreakers' yard at Dunston and on the 15th a fire at Cape Universal's factory, Bowburn, was attended by six pumps.

The Arcade, Chester-le-Street was well alight when the first crew from Fencehouses arrived. Fifteen pumps and two turntable ladders were required before the fire was brought under control.

Both Birtley water tenders and another Durham appliance at full stretch at the rear of the Arcade in Chester-le-Street in 1969.

One week later British Oxygen Co.'s plant at Vigo, Birtley, also required the attendance of six pumps. It was Newcastle's turn in December when fire raged through Callers Department Store, Northumberland Street in the city centre, just when the store was packed with goods for hungry Christmas shoppers. Fifteen pumps were ordered to this incident with the last appliance to attend coming from Hebburn. This was the first instance that an appliance from Durham County Fire Brigade had attended a fire within the city boundaries and nearly forty years would elapse before such an instance happened again.

Having adopted some form of standardisation for Bedford appliances, the 1969 order for water tender escapes and water tenders was awarded to HCB-Angus of Southampton for a batch of appliances based on Bedford KELZ3 6-ton chassis with 166bhp hi-performance petrol engines. Six body builders, HCB-Angus, Merryweather, Carmichael, Pyrene, Sun and Dennis, tendered for this order and whilst Merryweather's version, based on a Ford D600, was the cheapest, the contract was awarded to HCB-Angus's Bedford on account of the greater horse power of the engine. An additional emergency tender from HCB-Angus was also ordered for Framwellgate Moor but actually assigned to operate from Fencehouses. One appliance was written-off during the year, a Bedford water tender from Swallwell, which overturned near Scotswood Bridge whilst answering a fire call, fortunately without serious injury to the crew. Appliance

Sunderland Fire Brigade sent their turntable ladder to the Arcade fire at Chester-le-Street where it was positioned in a yard at the rear of the shops on the opposite side of the street so it could operate as a water tower.

Two firemen were injured when fire destroyed the Reeds Crane and Plant Hire factory at Blaydon-on-Tyne in August 1969. (*Newcastle Chronicle & Journal*)

conversions were still undertaken by the adept workshops staff and in 1969 a further two obsolete Commer water tenders were converted into foam tenders and assigned to Durham and Bishop Auckland. Whilst all of the operational appliances had been replaced during the previous twenty years, there were still three pre-war appliances in the fleet consisting of Leyland motor pumps, formerly of Stockton and Durham City Urban District Councils, and one Dennis appliance originally delivered to Bishop Auckland Council. In August the former Stockton Leyland limousine appliance with 60ft wheeled escape and traditional brass trim was sold at auction raising £123 in the process. Almost thirty years of age, the appliance, used by the training school, was still in first class operational condition and whilst it was a worthy candidate for preservation its whereabouts after disposal have never been ascertained. This left two pre-war appliances and two wartime conversions still operational but with their future existence in the brigade rapidly diminishing. In 1971 an approach was made by the director of Beamish Open Air Museum expressing an intention to open a fire brigade exhibition and museum housing appliances ranging from hand-operated pumps to more modern road appliances and suggested that when the old training school appliances were finally declared redundant they could be donated to the museum. The museum was fortunate in the request being complied with and the former Durham City Leyland Braidwood appliance, Bishop Auckland Dennis New World motor pump named *Aclet* and Hebburn's 1950 Dennis F12 pump escape were all handed over to the museum.

Newcastle & Gateshead Fire Service's biggest fire occurred at Callers Department Store, Northumberland Street, just before Christmas 1969. This was the first and only occasion that a pumping appliance from Durham County Fire Brigade was called in to the city centre. Here Hebburn's water tender, the fifteenth and last pump to attend, has just arrived in company with an appliance from Northumberland County Fire Brigade.

These were the last open-topped appliances to remain in use with any of the north-east fire brigades and have been fortunately preserved for posterity, but not in the way that was originally planned. All of the appliances were stored for many years and never formally displayed in the manner envisaged. The Dennis F12 later passed through the hands of three different preservationists, all committed to restoring the appliance back to its original state but, after languishing outside for many years after being released by the museum, it was determined that the cost of restoration was no longer viable and the machine was scrapped in April 1998, the spare parts being used by a similar appliance owned by Tyne & Wear Fire Brigade. However, an enterprising Sunderland fireman retained the front assembly, which was restored and reconstructed in his private garage. Currently the last remnants of Durham's first dual-purpose appliance are stored in a garage at Barnard Castle. The two pre-war appliances both passed to competent collectors and preservationists and will almost certainly re-appear restored to their original condition for future generations to appreciate the contrast between the appliances in use before the war and their modern streamlined, limousine counterparts.

The problem of the air-raid sirens sounding the alert for the brigade's part-time firemen to proceed to their stations and the complaints resulting from such alerts were finally being resolved, some twenty years after residents and councils first registered their complaints. In 1969 new pocket alerters (bleepers) were introduced for the on-call firemen that, as well as affording the advantages of enabling new retained firemen to commence on-call duties immediately and not inconvenience the general public with the wailing of the air-raid siren, the devices gave

In 1970 the brigade took delivery of a batch of Bedford TK appliances with HCB-Angus bodywork, one of which was completed with an unpainted natural aluminium finish. This was the sole Durham appliance to feature this type of livery. It served some of its time at Middleton in Teesdale. (I. Moore)

the firemen a whole new degree of freedom. With the siren call-out system the firemen were virtually tied to their houses or the immediate vicinity, within hearing distance of the siren, the sound of which could be affected by wind direction and traffic noise. The adoption of the pocket alerters cost three times the amount required for the existing system of sirens and call bells but in the interests of efficiency the system was introduced, initially at Sedgefield and Stanhope and in the succeeding years to all of the brigade's retained firemen. The sirens' mournful wails would sound no more! During the same period the control room was equipped with a new multi-phone system enabling messages to be passed simultaneously to all whole-time fire stations and a robophone machine that automatically recorded all messages transmitted by appliance wireless equipment.

Barnard Castle's new fire station was occupied on 29 October and at Chopwell the new fire station was occupied in November and officially opened in March 1970. Chopwell was the first new fire station to be built in Blaydon urban district's area. It was opened by Councillor Len Hawkshaw who, in 1939, was the first fire officer in charge of Chopwell Fire Brigade. Just four years later the station ceased to be part of Durham County Fire Brigade. Plans were also formulated and tenders released for a new day-manned fire station and ten houses at Middleton St George near Teesside Airport, presumably in place of the proposed Eaglescliffe development. The controversy regarding the implementation of day-manning arrangements at Seaham and other stations continued with the Fire Brigade Union vehemently resisting such developments and with the matter being forwarded to national level all such plans were deferred indefinitely.

This splendid former Stockton-on-Tees Leyland limousine pump escape had given over thirty years of service when sold by auction in 1972. Serving for many years at the training school, its present whereabouts has never been ascertained.

In 1972 Beamish Open Air Museum acquired three redundant appliances from Durham including this former Durham City Leyland Braidwood motor pump pictured here in 1968 when in use with the training school at Framwellgate Moor.

Also donated to Beamish Open Air Museum was the former Bishop Auckland Dennis new world-style motor pump. Named *Aclet*, this was the only named appliance in the post-war Durham fleet and is pictured on a sombre occasion.

Ten houses had already been completed at Seaham and a similar amount for the personnel at Washington's new station, at which there was little residential accommodation. Two of the houses at Washington were used for the officer in charge and for dormitory accommodation; the remainder and all of the houses at Seaham were boarded up until the matter could be resolved. The building works at Middleton St George were also deferred and consideration was given to an alternative site at Gainford. Apart from Newton Aycliffe, the day-manning system was not developed any further in Durham and the houses at Seaham and Washington were eventually sold to the respective councils for use by other residents, apart from the two used by the firemen at Washington. Also in 1970 a new VF (Voice Frequency) (System A) communication system was introduced whereby central mobilising, initially at twelve fire stations, enabled all fire calls to be received by brigade control instead of the nearest fire station, where one of the operational firemen was detailed to man the watchroom and to receive fire calls and turn out the appliances, not only for his own fire station but in some cases for some of the surrounding retained fire stations. The centralised receipt of fire calls negated the need for firemen to permanently man watchrooms. In the previous twelve months, up to 31 March 1970, the brigade attended 2,038 property fires, 1,031 chimneys, 723 grass and heath and 196 special service calls. The uniformed personnel numbered 351 whole-time against an authorised establishment of 380, together with a total of 256 retained firefighters.

South Shields fireboat, for which Durham County Council contributed a share of the operating costs, was put to good use in September 1970 when the Cypriot motor ship *Petros*, and its cargo of 2,550 tons of timber pit props, lying off Mercantile dry dock Jarrow caught fire. Six of the crew of twenty-three, including the captain's wife, required hospitalisation and crews from

Barnard Castle inhabited this fire station in 1969. Pictured in 2003 is the station's brace of Dennis appliances, a Sabre and a Rapier.

It was 1963 before the site of new headquarters was fully occupied, the last part being the training school accommodation at the extreme east end. Apart from the doors to the appliance room, the external appearance remains little changed to this day.

Northumberland County Fire Brigade, who assisted Durham's fire crews, were transferred to the boat by breeches buoys and small craft. In October, Ferryhill's retained crew were first to attend a fire and explosion at Bailes Garage that required a total of ten pumps before it was brought under control. During the fire the Essoldo Bingo Hall next door had to be swiftly evacuated and windows were shattered in several houses, a newsagents shop and the Kings Head Hotel. Three firemen were injured after becoming trapped between two manoeuvring fire engines. The garage, which was completely blown to bits, and six cars were no more. A particularly interesting call occurred on 8 January involving the mobilisation of resources from both Durham and Northumberland fire brigades. One of the Royal Air Force's 'V' bomber force aircraft, a huge delta wing Avro Vulcan aircraft from 44 Squadron, Waddington, Lincolnshire, suffered a major engine fire whilst over the north-eastern counties, resulting in a large number of fire calls being placed with the local fire brigades. After a gallant effort to reach a diversionary airfield at Leeming, the crew were forced to abandon the aircraft, three of them doing so over Otterburn, whereupon the aircraft nose-dived to the ground in a field at Wingate leaving a crater 25ft deep, remarkably without any loss of life or injury. For his leadership and airmanship the pilot, Flight Lieutenant Alcock was awarded the Air Force Cross. Ironically the same pilot was in charge of a similar aircraft that was unfortunate enough to crash at Malta some four years later. Another ship fire occurred in April 1972, two years after the *Petros* fire, when the MV *Teesdale H*, a bunkering tanker berthed at Shell Mex, Jarrow, suffered a fire in the accommodation area to which five pumps responded. With great diligence the fire was prevented from spreading, but so severe was the damage sustained that this factor, together with the age of the vessel, meant it was declared a constructive total loss and was ignominiously towed up to Clayton-Davy Shipbreakers yard, Dunston-on-Tyne for scrapping. Coincidentally this same yard was responsible for scrapping some of the old appliances that had served with Durham County Fire Brigade in the immediate post-war years.

In March 1971, five new water tenders and two dual-purpose appliances were ordered, the resultant tenders prompting a complete change from the types of appliances previously ordered. The lowest tender was submitted by Ford for an appliance with a Canadian Ford engine but, because of difficulties envisaged with spare parts and better performance from the second highest tender, the next generation of appliances were ordered from Dennis Bros, Guildford, the first Dennis pumping appliances to be purchased since 1954. This type of appliance, the Dennis 'D' model was, apart from the Jaguar 4.2-litre petrol engine fitted into the first batches, completely produced in-house and, apart from the odd exception, formed the basis of the appliance fleet for the next decade and beyond. Five more were ordered the next year following the successful evaluation of the previous batch, two of them being fitted to carry a Hathaway portable pump. Also ordered this year was a totally new type of appliance, a hydraulic platform vehicle or Simon Snorkel, an appliance complementary to the turntable ladders and comprised of an ERF chassis on which was mounted a set of hydraulically operated booms with a cage on top, capable of being elevated to a height of 85ft. Similar appliances were already in use with Darlington and Newcastle & Gateshead fire services. One appliance was prematurely lost from the fleet in March when Hebburn's recently delivered Bedford water tender escape overturned and caught fire on Albert Road, Jarrow, whilst en route to a fire. The appliance was written-off but the actions of the crew prompted the Fire Brigade Committee to place on record their appreciation of the comradeship, courage and initiative displayed by the Hebburn personnel at that incident. The days of the old wheeled escapes were drawing to an end at this time with the design appearing likely to go out of production in the near future and with the increasing popularity of new light-alloy triple-extension ladders. Seven of these new ladders were ordered from Angus Fire Armour in April 1972 for fitting to the new Dennis appliances. These appliances were the last

From 1971 onwards appliances manufactured by Dennis were adopted as the standard form of pumping appliances in the Durham fleet. This early Jaguar-powered Dennis D-type water tender with 45ft light-alloy ladder was one of seven such appliances delivered in 1972.

in the brigade to be fitted with the traditional fire bell. No more wheeled escapes were ordered, although the mixture of John Morris wooden escapes and Merryweather steel escapes had a few years of life left in them yet.

Assistant Chief Fire Officer Bill Hagan, who had recently been awarded the Queen's Fire Service Medal, retired at the beginning of December to enjoy almost thirty years of retirement until he passed away in 2001 aged eighty-eight years. From the four external and two internal applicants for the post, Divisional Officer William Tozer, son of the brigade's first assistant chief fire officer, Charles Tozer, was promoted internally as the new second-in-command.

Fires of note were Morganite Resistors, Bede Trading Estate, Jarrow, on 10 February, at which twelve jets and two turntable ladder monitors were used for a fire that destroyed a large single-storey building. Appliances from South Shields and Newcastle & Gateshead fire brigades supported the Hebburn crews. Almost one month later, 100 firemen with ten pumping appliances from Durham County, South Shields, Newcastle & Gateshead and Northumberland were mobilised to an early morning blaze at Lennigs Chemicals, Jarrow, where a two-storey building containing various chemicals was destroyed by fire. Under the command of Divisional Officer W. Tozer, a total of fifteen jets were brought to bear on the fire. Other large fires of the year occurred at Thompson's Farm, Tindal Crescent (eight pumps), Shearex Plastics, Spennymoor (six pumps) and Old Acres Hall Farm, Butterwick (twelve pumps). The old Tivoli

Hebburn's new Bedford water tender escape did not last long. It was written-off after overturning and catching fire whilst on its way to a fire call, thankfully without serious injury to any of the crew. (D. Barker)

Cinema on Park Road, Southmoor, Stanley, was attended to by six pumps in November. It was a wonder that the place was still standing for, in July 1964, six pumps were called to the building and seven years before that a similar attendance had to be called for to extinguish a serious fire in the building.

The old wartime control unit and canteen van conversions were withdrawn in 1972 after giving over twenty years of service and, following auction at Central Motor Auctions, Maltby, both passed into the hands of preservationists. Both are still extant, the control unit stored in premises not too far away from its original base at Felling-on-Tyne. The replacement appliances, from Adams & Gibbons Ltd with coachwork by Northern Assemblies, were both based on Bedford coach chassis. The control unit featured three separate compartments; the first was equipped with mobilising boards and full communication facilities including intrinsically safe pocket radio sets, portable radio sets, a ten-channel radio set, telephone switchboard with three extensions for field telephones, together with a PA system and tape recorder and two retractable 30ft masts operated by compressed air. The centre compartment contained conference facilities with blackboards, large-scale maps and seats which could be made into beds, whilst the rearmost compartment contained washing and toilet facilities. Two multi-reflector flashing lights were fitted on the roof, the blue reflectors used for travelling to incidents and on arrival the red and white reflectors were used, readily identifying the unit as the incident control point.

Ten pumps were called to this fire at Lennig Chemical Works, Jarrow, in March 1971. Firemen from the county are in the process of extinguishing any remaining hot spots during the aftermath of the blaze. (*Newcastle Chronicle & Journal*)

The canteen van, based on an identical unit and said to be the best of its type in the country, had catering facilities for supplying a full range of hot meals for up to 100 personnel and contained seating facilities for up to eighteen. Both were assigned to Framwellgate Moor. An extra addition to the fleet was a pump carrier, later re-designated 'water relay unit', a converted 1964 Commer workshops' service van adapted to carry portable pumps and extra hose for use at fires, notably in rural areas where water supplies were poor. On order were two new concept appliances: a pump/hydraulic platform appliance, which was basically a standard water tender with the addition of a 50ft Simon Snorkel elevating platform, ordered as a replacement for one of the escape appliances, and the second, a 'Simonitor' appliance, also a water tender but equipped with an elevating 50ft boom on which was attached a monitor, remote-controlled from ground level, and an escape ladder. This appliance, equipped with a 1,000gpm pump, was ordered as a replacement for a ladder appliance. The hydraulically operated boom could be elevated to a

Her Majesty's Inspector of Fire Services, Mr Bidgood, was most complementary during the 1973 annual inspection, especially towards the brigade's personnel welfare commitments with the new mobile canteen van, pictured here at Framwellgate Moor soon after delivery.

maximum height of 50ft and a maximum horizontal outreach of 42ft and during rescue work was capable of supporting four men on the escape ladder attached to the boom, which could be operated from ground level or a duplicate set of controls at the boom tip. Both appliances were mounted on Dennis chassis powered by Rolls-Royce B81 engines with automatic transmission. These types of appliances, adopted by many fire brigades, were the latest developments in fire-fighting and were envisaged as being the appliances of the future. In reality this was not the case and the notion of pumps with hydraulic platform equipment was not pursued any further. Both the Durham appliances were short-lived and were both out of service by 1984 but, ironically, the hydraulic platform appliance was still in service in southern Ireland in 2006! Crook and Ferryhill Fire Stations were upgraded to two-pump status, all manned by retained personnel; the additional appliances utilising former bays previously assigned to the Auxiliary Fire Service.

Retained Station Officer Coffield of Sedgefield Fire Station received the British Empire Medal in 1972 and joined Station Officer H.R. Horner who received a similar award in 1968. A meeting of the region's chief fire officers took place in Durham in July to discuss plans being proposed for the formation of a new brigade for the Tyne & Wear region and also to formulate the general arrangements of men and appliances for the new area, plus to be of assistance to the new authority when it was elected. A Local Government Reorganisation Act was pending which proposed the establishment of a number of new counties, the abolition of several existing counties and the incorporation into the new counties of the separate county boroughs.

A publicity line-up in the rear yard at Framwellgate Moor of four Dennis D-type water tender/ladders and the Dennis F49 Simonitor and hydraulic platform appliances that were delivered in 1973.

If it went ahead, the reorganisation would mean that Durham County Fire Brigade would be handing over one fifth of its manpower and appliances to the new Tyne & Wear Metropolitan County, further decreasing the size of the brigade following the previous transferring of Hartlepool and Stockton Fire Stations in 1967 and 1968.

Malicious false alarms, the calling out of the fire brigade to none existent incidents, remained an increasing problem for not only Durham County Fire Brigade but for the country as a whole. The problem was first raised in 1972, when nationally 9.6 per cent of all calls were of malicious origin. In the years 1970–71 the brigade was called out to malicious calls on 524 occasions; in 1972–73 the total had risen to 997 representing 12 per cent of the total calls in the county compared to 3.3 per cent of the total calls in 1948–49. In 1971 the brigade had been able to trace only twenty-seven persons making such calls, of which proceedings were taken against twelve. The type of people behind the influx of calls were said to be 'irresponsible or malicious anti-social adults with problems of low morality or drunk' and 'undisciplined and misguided children and adolescents who do not appreciate the potential consequences of their activities'. A large proportion of the calls were from children aged below ten years old and many others aged between ten and fourteen. The facility of voice recording equipment in the brigade control room appeared to be no deterrent and did not increase the detection rate. After much debate it was determined that there appeared to be no answer to the problem except that when the culprit was apprehended more severe punishment should result. Usually the maximum £15 penalty and/or three months' imprisonment was not fully imposed. Of the many genuine calls three schools suffered serious fires in 1972, all in Hebburn's area in the north of the county: County Clegwell School, Mountbatten Avenue, Hebburn in April; Highfield Comprehensive School, Felling in August and Falla Park Junior School, Felling in October. Damage to the second-floor science block at Highfield Comprehensive School amounted to over £200,000. The new canteen van and control unit had their baptism of fire at this incident – the appliances were only ten days

The sole pump/hydraulic platform appliance in Durham had a life span of just over ten years before being sold for further service in the Republic of Ireland. It was still in service there in 2006, over twenty years after first being withdrawn. (M. Forsyth)

old when turned out to this fire. The same school was later the scene of a fifteen-pump fire in the days when the area came under the jurisdiction of Tyne & Wear Metropolitan Fire Brigade. Scots House Farm, Boldon, also in Hebburn's area, required an attendance of nine pumps on 11 November and was the precursor of a spate of farm fires in the early quarter of 1973 which required attendances of five or more pumps. Hill Head Farm, Sunniside, was a victim in February and in March, High Hill House Farm, Ferryhill, Hough Hall Farm, Quarrington and Finchale Banks Farm, Leamside, all suffered losses to haystacks and barns. More schools fell prey to the ravages of fire: Hall Lane Modern School, Houghton-le-Spring, required six pumps in March and in May a fire in the kitchens and dining hall at Lord Lawson School, Birtley, was attended by eight pumps. The retained unit at Birtley was busy again in August when six pumps were called to a fire at Durham Chemicals, Mary Avenue, Birtley. The previous day, at the same site, a fire in the decanting plant that contained drums of highly inflammable liquid was severely damaged and required the attendance of a total of twelve pumps and a foam tender! These premises were at the end of the street on which Birtley Fire Station was situated and some of the firemen were actually employed at the site. Young's Motors, Chester-le-Street, also had its second big fire when another load of tyres waiting re-treading caught fire.

The visit of Her Majesty's Inspector of Fire Services was still an annual event and in May 1973, following a visit by Inspector Bidgood, extreme satisfaction was recorded regarding the standards of efficiency inherent in the brigade. It was further expressed that Durham County Fire Brigade led the country with its communications systems, were pioneers in personnel welfare with the canteen van and were amongst the best-equipped brigades in the country. Stanley's new fire station, built on the same site as the existing one, was opened in October 1973 and the same year the brigade's retained firemen won the battle to lower the age of retirement to fifty-five years in line with the whole-time firemen. Despite the ruling and because of the problems in recruiting suitable applicants, firemen above this age – notably in the upper Weardale region where two firemen at Middleton in Teesdale exceeded the grand age of sixty-five, one of them approaching seventy years of age and eight others aged between fifty-five and sixty years at other locations – were permitted to remain on the rolls providing annual medical examinations by the brigade doctor proved satisfactory. Despite the ages of some of the 'pensioner firemen' in the retained section of the brigade, it was alleged that Middleton in Teesdale was the fastest turning-out retained station in the country! The following year the two stalwarts, Messrs Robinson and Walton at Middleton in Teesdale, gracefully retired after having served at the station since the formation of the county fire brigade.

Over the years some of the edges of the county of Durham had slowly been whittled away; Hartlepool's fire station transferred into the West Hartlepool brigade in 1967 and a year later Stockton's fire station became part of Teesside County Borough. The further changes and mergers, discussed in 1972, that proposed the abolishment of some of the country's counties and the establishment of new counties and metropolitan counties was implemented in 1974 and, as predicted, Durham County Fire Brigade did not escape the changes. At midnight on 31 March 1974 the northern-most fire stations at Birtley, Chopwell, Hebburn, Swallwell and Washington, all relatively newly constructed premises, and their personnel and appliances became part of the new Tyne & Wear Metropolitan County. One hundred officers and men and twelve appliances ceased to be part of Durham County Council. At the same time, and perhaps as some sort of compensatory measure, the county borough of Darlington's fire brigade and a small part of the North Riding of Yorkshire excluding any fire stations were incorporated into the county of Durham. One fire station, an ultra-modern building built in 1973 and situated on the inner ring road, and fifty-five Darlington officers and men were incorporated into Durham County Fire Brigade. In the transfer of the new Tyne & Wear personnel Chief Fire Officer Walker, who became an Officer of the Order of the British Empire (OBE) in June, expressed his admiration for how 'their sterling service over the years assisted in no small measure to the attainment of that high level of efficiency of the brigade as a whole to which we are all justly proud'! The revised personnel establishment in the county was now 438 uniformed officers and men, 270 part-time/retained firefighters and ninety-five civilian administration and ancillary staff. Mutual aid schemes between Durham and the defunct brigades of Newcastle & Gateshead, South Shields, Sunderland and Teesside were terminated as a result of the mergers and new agreements were made between Tyne & Wear Fire Brigade and Cleveland Fire Brigade and the part-funding of the South Shields fireboat was also withdrawn as the industrial parts of the south side of the river Tyne now fell wholly within the jurisdiction of the Tyne & Wear fire authority.

The county's biggest fire after the 1965 ICI incident occurred in August 1974 at Consett Distillation Works where an 18-acre site, on which was stored some 3,000 45-gallon drums of petroleum-based solvents such as Acetone, Toluene, Xylene, White Spirit and cellulose thinners, became heavily involved in fire. The site concerned consisted of a compound containing bulk storage tanks, a drum storage area and a distillation tower with a separately owned neighbouring factory that also contained flammable liquids in an adjoining storage area. The first call to the fire was raised at just before 10 a.m. whereupon it became evident to the officer in charge of the first appliance that a serious fire situation was in progress and reinforcing appliances were ordered whilst en route to the fire. Within 45 minutes of the call, twenty pumps had been mobilised to

The oldest appliance to be inherited by the county fire brigade in the 1974 re-organisation was Darlington's 1951 Dennis F12 pump escape, which was sold in 1978 and promptly scrapped. Note the '999' registration that was common to all Darlington fire engines.

the fire where crews were hampered in the early stages by a shortage of water in the immediate vicinity of the compound coupled with drums being stored right up against the compound fence, allowing fire to spread into the adjoining factory drum storage area. The fire was intensified and spread in all directions by drums exploding and being projected considerable distances, presenting a major hazard to fire-fighting personnel. Fire-fighting was concentrated on the prevention of spread to adjoining factory buildings and six 3,000-gallon and three 5,000-gallon tanks containing solvents. 425 gallons of foam compound were used at the incident which was extinguished by ten jets and one foam branch. The fire was discovered by a forklift truck driver who was engaged in restacking 5-gallon drums of 'blue flash', a liquid recovered from the process of putting the blue coating in photographic flash bulbs. Within a short time dozens of drums were involved, many of them exploding and catapulting up to 200ft in the air. A pall of smoke rising up to 1,000ft in the air was visible from a distance of 12 miles. In a statement made by Chief Fire Office Walker, the drums were exploding and blowing others in the air causing firemen to leave hoses and run for cover as they rained down like mortar shells. The explosions could be heard as far away as Gateshead, a distance of 12 miles, and was described as reminiscent of an artillery barrage. This was the plant's first fire in five years and took the brigade five hours to bring it under control

The joint turn-out arrangements between Durham County Fire Brigade and Newcastle & Gateshead Joint Fire Service were terminated in April 1974, following the Local Government Re-organisation Act. Swallwell's water tender is seen attending a garden shed fire at Low Teams, Gateshead, shortly before being relieved by crews from Gateshead Fire Station in whose area the fire originated.

Swalwell's water tender escape had a few more years of service after the re-organisation of 1974 and is pictured at the site of the new Freeman Road Hospital, operating without the wheeled escape, which had all been withdrawn from service by Tyne & Wear Metropolitan Fire Brigade.

The spectacular fire at Consett Distillations in August 1974, at which many explosions of chemical drums took place, remains one of the county's biggest fires of all time.

using 120 men and twenty-five pumping appliances. In the Consett distillation compound severe damage was caused to 6,000 45-gallon and 5-gallons drums of various solvents, several bulk tanks containing some 25,000 gallons of solvents, two small prefabricated offices, pump house, two forklift trucks, a motor lorry, a 28ft trailer and a self-propelled grooving machine. The distillation tower was slightly damaged. In the Thomas Swan compound some 600 45-gallon drums of various flammable liquids were severely damaged. To date the appliances and manpower mobilised to this fire has fortunately never been exceeded. In September ten pumps attended a lunchtime fire at Doggarts department store in the centre of Durham City when fire damaged four rooms on the fourth floor. Crews wearing breathing apparatus entered the store to make sure no one was trapped inside but, fortunately, the building had been evacuated without injury to either staff or customers. This was the first fire that the brigade's new Simonitor appliance had attended. The Consett area was the scene again of the county's next biggest fire when the four-year-old premises of George and R. Dewhurst's man-made fibre manufacturer at Leadgate caught fire at 4.30 a.m. Over 200 tons of baled raw materials and finishing yarns were lost during the fire, which took two hours to bring under control and was hampered by the vast amounts of smoke, terrific heat and the gases being given off by the fibres.

Concern was expressed that year regarding the amount of sick leave and time taken off by the county's firemen, prompting the County Management Service Unit to carry out an investigation following claims made by the Fire Brigade Union that the brigade was undermanned. The Durham branch of the union was asking for seventy-four extra firemen and twenty-five other officer ranks amid allegations that special appliances were sometimes unmanned and men were unable to take leave or attend courses. In reply the chief fire officer stated that the current establishment against the background of fire risk was adequate but the committee may, as a matter of policy, decide to increase the level of manning. The go-ahead was given, however, for the recruitment of an additional forty-eight members of staff and two fire prevention officers for when the firemen's working week was reduced from fifty-six hours to forty-eight hours in November.

The mid-1970s saw a spate of school fires occurring in the Durham and Tyne & Wear areas; Elmfield Junior School, Newton Hall, being the thirty-ninth such blaze in the north in one year, 1975. The fortieth was at Greenlands Infant School, South Moor, on 13 February. Appliances attended this early morning fire from Stanley, Consett, Durham, Langley Park and Fencehouses. In September the kitchens and a range of classrooms at Pelton Roseberry School near Chester-le-Street were damaged in a fire to which twelve pumps, including one from Tyne & Wear Fire Brigade, responded. Two thirds of the main school building was well alight on the arrival of the fire brigade. This was the fifth fire at this particular school in less than twelve months. In October 1974 ten pumps attended a fire that caused £200,000 damage to the science laboratories and classrooms and just two weeks later another fire saw damage, estimated at £75,000, caused to the technical block and gymnasium. On Guy Fawkes Night a fire in a book cupboard in the sixth form block was discovered by cleaners and in May 1975 another fire was discovered in the boys' toilets but was extinguished by staff before the arrival of the fire brigade. A fifteen-year-old boy was later ordered to be detained for a maximum of seven years for starting one of the blazes, the judge stating that the boy was a serious risk to the public and the blaze was a deliberate, planned, ingenious and dangerous act of arson. In November four firefighters received injuries that necessitated hospital treatment whilst fighting a fire at the disused Essoldo Cinema, Chester-le-Street. Ten pumps, including one from Tyne & Wear, attended this incident. Fires involving farm outbuildings and barns, often in remote areas with restricted water supplies, are annual features of all rural fire brigades and the rural aspects of the county of Durham were no exception. In August 1975 ten pumps attended a fire at Fold House Farm, Howden-le-Wear, where a range of farm buildings, including the farmhouse, a stone barn and cow shed and a four-bay Dutch barn, were all involved in fire. The disused Variety Club at Clarence Street, Spennymoor, was destroyed in a fire that required an attendance of ten pumps, a turntable ladder and hydraulic platform. On the arrival of the first crews flames were shooting 60ft into the air, every door was alight and the wooden roof supports and floors were burning fiercely. Known as 'The Rink' in its dance hall days, the premises were on the sale market by Vaux Breweries. A fire involving two furniture-type vans, laden with consignments of fur fabrics, at Haward & Robertson's Garden Street premises, Darlington, caught firefighters unawares and ten crew members had to be admitted to hospital suffering from the effects of toxic fumes, of which two were detained overnight, fortunately with no lasting effects. The total number of fire calls for the previous year, April 1975–April 1976 was 5,322, of which 877 were chimneys. This was a reduction from the previous year's figures because of the transfer of fire stations to the new Tyne & Wear authority.

Durham County Fire Brigade was the first brigade in the area to request the Home Office provide inter-brigade wireless equipment to enable a radio communication network to be established between the individual fire brigades of Cleveland, Cumberland, Northumberland,

Pelton Roseberry School near Chester-le-Street was the scene of several fires in 1975. The fifth such event depicted here shows one of the classrooms at the school heavily involved in fire. (*Newcastle Chronicle & Journal*)

North Yorkshire and Tyne & Wear, particularly in the cases of major incidents. A new call-out system was also introduced at Stanley and Durham Fire Stations where crews could now be alerted and called out by a PA system, through which messages and fire calls could be broadcast throughout the stations, speeding up the turnout times. A fire appliance at Teesside Airport was fitted with a wireless set tuned to the county fire brigade's frequency so that the airport fire brigade and the control room and mobiles in the county could communicate with each other. The scheme to equip all retained personnel with pocket alerters was completed, by which time 262 firemen from sixteen fire stations were so equipped. The call bells, attached to the homes of the on-call firemen, were all gradually removed and at last, after almost thirty years of sounding their mournful wails, the air-raid siren system was declared redundant.

The year 1976 was one of the hottest and driest on record and consequently resulted in an inordinate amount of additional calls to fires involving grass, hedgerows and crops due to prolonged drought conditions. There was a 27 per cent increase in false alarms and fires, the second biggest increase in the history of the brigade. The daily average of calls doubled and in August 1,400 calls were dealt with. Regularly during the month the brigade was dealing with between eighty and 100 calls each day and in one single day alone the brigade attended over 100 calls. At one stage thirty of the brigade's thirty-six pumps were engaged in fighting fires. A large number of farm fires were recorded and hundreds of acres of crops went up in smoke. Ten pumps were used at a forest fire at Indian Farm near Crook and at Eppleby 61 hectares of stubble and straw were burnt. Seven appliances were required at Embleton Old Farm where a Dutch barn and its contents of 150 tons of baled straw were destroyed. There were eighteen other fires involving hay barns and farm outbuildings. Shearex Plastics, Spennymoor, the site of a previous fire in 1971, was involved in another blaze in June 1976 that was described as being the biggest fire in the town since 1929 when Kenmire's furniture factory – ironically situated on the same site – burned to the ground. It was the third fire at the works in the month and on this occasion flames were through the roof by the time the fire brigade arrived; smoke emitting from the incident was visible from 10 miles away. Residents were evacuated from Oak Terrace and so many hundreds of local people turned out to watch the proceedings that an enterprising ice cream van took the opportunity to secure some additional trade. On the same day the brigade tackled another serious fire, at Woodhead Steel factory, Aycliffe Industrial Estate, which was rocked by three bangs as gas cylinders, stored in the building, exploded. The total calls for the year numbered 6,099, 1,279 being to grass and gorse fires. Sub-Officer G.E. Cartmell of Langley Park and members from Framwellgate Moor Fire Station were awarded the RSPCA's Certificate of Merit for their courage and humanity in rescuing seventeen beasts and a colt trapped in a Byre at Square House Farm, Quebec, in February and later in the year the Royal Humane Society's testimonial on Vellum was awarded to J.R. Whaley, divisional officer of the south division, for his part in the rescue of two boys from a slurry pond at Witton Park.

April 1977 saw the brigade attend another major fire, this time at the premises of Smart & Browns, Spennymoor, where a range of single-storey buildings used for the manufacturing of

There were two serious fires at Shearex Plastics, Spennymoor. This is the first one that occurred in 1976 and shows former Swallwell Bedford water tender and Durham's 85ft hydraulic platform. (*Newcastle Chronicle & Journal*)

electric cookers was severely damaged by fire. Fifteen pumps attended this fire. On 1 May eight appliances attended a fire at Trimdon Colliery Working Men's Club.

The brigade's workshop was still adept at vehicle conversions and in 1977 a redundant emergency tender from Peterlee was converted into a combined breathing apparatus/decontamination unit, equipped with twelve positive pressure breathing apparatus sets, showers, protective clothing and other equipment for undertaking the decontamination of brigade personnel whilst attending incidents involving chemicals. The appliance was assigned to Darlington.

On 14 November 1977 an unprecedented act in the history of the British fire service occurred when the nation's firefighters, in support of a £20 per week pay rise and a reduction in the working week and in opposition to the Government's maximum 10 per cent pay increase, withdrew their labour and consequently the first fire service's national strike began. Fire cover in the county, and throughout most of the British Isles, was provided by personnel from the Army, Royal Navy and Royal Air Force, supported by the police. Hundreds of stored former AFS green goddess emergency pumps were made ready for use, armed forces personnel hastily trained and subsequently allocated to bases at various police stations, hospitals and Territorial Army Camps. In Durham a total of 160 troops and ten green goddesses were allocated, two each to Army drill halls at Durham City, Horden, Darlington, Bishop Auckland and Stanley. The county council's underground bunker at County Hall, formerly set up as a wartime emergency centre, was used by the army as their communications headquarters. Some part-time fire stations continued to provide cover in their own station areas but, apart from these, the armed forces were the sole providers of fire protection in the country until the strike was resolved and normal cover resumed on 15 January, the following year. On the eve of the strike part-time firemen at Barnard Castle turned in to respond to a report of a car fire to find that both appliances had flat batteries. The crews had to drive to the scene on the A67 near Bowes in a private car then run to a nearby farmhouse to fetch buckets of water to put out the fire. Chief Inspector Derek Harrison of Barnard Castle police station said, 'Sabotaging had been carried out by someone familiar with fire engines'. One theory suggested at the time was that the alleged sabotage might have been carried out before the men agreed at the weekend to support the strike call. At the car fire the police were on scene and attempted to extinguish the fire with hand extinguishers before the firemen arrived, much to the surprise of the car owners who 'expected a big red fire engine not just a little car with four men and a couple of buckets.' Such is the ingenuity of firefighters! During the eight weeks that the dispute lasted the military attended 535 incidents, 99.4 per cent of the total fires recorded.

Chief Fire Officer Duncan Walker retired in 1979 and was succeeded by former Durham County firefighter T.F. (Fred) Elton, by then an assistant chief fire officer with Tyne & Wear Metropolitan Fire Brigade. His tenure was short-lived, for two years later he moved back to Tyne & Wear to command the brigade as chief fire officer. In 1979 the firemen's working week was reduced from 44 hours to 42 hours, necessitating the introduction of a fourth watch – the green watch – to add to the already established red, white and blue watches. This extra 'shift' prompted a whole new campaign to recruit additional firemen and junior fire officers. Fire control room operator, Miss Joan Coulson, who had recently completed twenty-five years of service, was awarded the British Empire Medal in 1979. Presented by the Lord Lieutenant, Lord Barnard, his citation read:

She has always been ready to take on additional responsibilities far exceeding of her work which was demonstrated on several occasions when dealing with exceptional incidents in which life had been at risk.

Fifteen pumping appliances and an assortment of special appliances were required at Smart & Browns Spennymoor factory fire in 1977. Durham's 85ft 'Simon Snorkel' appliance is pictured at the scene together with Fencehouses's emergency tender and Durham's control unit.

During the national fire fighters' dispute, Dawdon Club, Seaham – recently re-opened after a previous fire – was the scene of another serious fire to which the Army was called to attend using green goddess emergency pumps.

One fire of note that year was at Durham City's bus depot in the early hours of Sunday 22 July when residents, alerted by the sound of exploding tyres, became aware of a raging fire inside. On the arrival of the first crews it was discovered that eight buses at the rear of the garage were well alight threatening a 6,000-gallon diesel tank, a severe explosion hazard. Efforts to remove fifty buses parked very close to each other inside the garage by firefighters and police were hampered by the fact that there were five different methods of starting the vehicles and several had to have small fires extinguished as they were driven out. By the time the fire was extinguished, fifteen buses and 10 per cent of the roof of the depot were severely damaged.

Fifteen pumps were called to a timber yard fire at Darlington on 11 May 1980, where stacks of timber 12ft high, covering an area of 100x150 metres, aided by fresh north-westerly winds and a previous long dry spell of weather, blazed furiously, threatening to spread to nearby sawmills and offices within the yard. Occurring at 12.30 p.m., the fire was brought under control some three hours later with the aid of nine jets and a half-mile twin-line water relay, set up with the aid of the recently commissioned new water relay unit appliance. The biggest fire of 1981 and the worst in south Durham since the war occurred on 27 August when fire severely damaged the premises of Thorn EMI, Spennymoor Industrial Estate. The building was only five years old and the fire was reported to have started in the centre of a stack of corrugated cardboard packages shortly before midday. Within a short time the whole of the premises was involved in fire despite attempts by works brigade personnel to extinguish the fire using two hose lines.

Left: Mr T.F. Elton was appointed chief fire officer in 1979 after the retirement of Duncan Walker. Within two years Mr Elton had moved on to become chief fire officer of Tyne & Wear Metropolitan Fire Brigade.

Opposite: Terry Malpas, assistant chief fire officer of Bedfordshire, was appointed to the position of chief fire officer of Durham in 1982 and commanded the brigade until his retirement in 1990.

As the fire progressed fourteen jets of water were played on the fire but such was the rapidity of fire spread that the roof collapsed and the entire contents were destroyed, Damage at this fire was estimated at £8,500,000. Senior Divisional Officer Stanger took charge of the operations using twenty pumps and six special appliances. Crews and appliances from Tyne & Wear stood in at fire stations at Consett, Fencehouses and Stanley and Cleveland provided cover at Peterlee and Seaham.

In 1982, Mr Terry Malpas, the assistant chief fire officer of Bedfordshire Fire Brigade, was appointed as the new chief fire officer of Durham County Fire Brigade upon Mr T.F. Elton securing the chief fire officer's post in Tyne & Wear. A former Royal Navy clearance diver, Mr Malpas commenced his fire service career in 1967 with Bradford City Fire Brigade and, following various moves, he attained the rank of assistant chief fire officer in Bedfordshire before securing the chief fire officer's post in Durham. He remained in office until his retirement in August 1990.

A tragic event in the history of peacetime fire-fighting in the county of Durham occurred on the night of Saturday 4 September 1982 when a fire appliance from Peterlee, en route to a chimney fire in South Hetton, left the carriageway on the Easington to South Hetton road during rainy weather conditions and overturned into a deep trench at the side of the road. Of the five-man crew, two young firefighters, John Donley and Tony Hall, were trapped underneath the wreckage and despite heroic efforts from their own colleagues and those from the other stations swiftly mobilised to the incident – including crews with both of the brigades' breakdown vehicles – they both tragically succumbed to their injuries. This unfortunate incident remains a painful reminder of the risks inherent, not just from fire, but prevalent in the day-to-day working of the fire service. Lessons are invariably learned from such tragedies and as a result it

was decided that all future fire appliances would be diesel powered with automatic transmissions and ABS braking systems fitted and would feature strengthened crew cabs. This was the end of any further deliveries of the fibreglass-cabbed Dennis D appliances that had been a feature of the brigade since the first one was delivered in 1971. The next appliances delivered came from Dennis but were larger SS133 series appliances with reinforced steel cabs and assigned to Consett (two) and Durham. In 1984 a complete change in the type of water tenders employed in the county occurred when, after a long line of Dennis-made vehicles, four Bedford TK1269 chassis with bodywork by Mountain Range Ltd were delivered and assigned initially in pairs to Peterlee and Seaham. At the time Dennis appliances did not meet the specifications required by Durham County Fire Brigade and thus a one-off order was placed with Bedford for the 1983–84 appliance replacement program. For the following years Dennis, by now renamed Hestair-Dennis, was able to supply a new type of vehicle on the 7ft-wide 'DS' chassis and thereafter Dennis vehicles became the norm again with several batches of Dennis steel safety-cabbed DS151 appliances being delivered with bodywork constructed by various coachbuilders, including Dennis, Carmichael and the Scottish firm of Fulton & Wylie. Two new 100ft-turntable ladders were also delivered, both mounted onto Dennis chassis with ladders made by Magirus of Germany, the same company that had supplied the ladder to the deposed Framwellgate Moor appliance. The new turntable ladders resulted in the former borough of Darlington's unusual Leyland Firemaster being withdrawn. The Firemaster chassis was Leyland's attempt to regain a stronghold in the post-war fire appliance scene but to no avail and only a dozen such vehicles were built, including one other turntable ladder for Wolverhampton Fire Brigade. The former Darlington example has been preserved. The Durham Dennis-Magirus appliance, withdrawn after the replacement vehicle was delivered, had a rather chequered career after disposal; it was sold to Kent Fire Brigade in 1985 for further use and was last noted lying derelict in a scrap yard in Gloucestershire in 1989.

Deputy Chief Fire Officer William (Bill) Tozer, the son of the original assistant chief fire officer of Durham, Charles Tozer, retired in 1984 after having served a total of thirty-five years in the fire service, all within the county of Durham and thus ending a long line of fire service Tozers. The last of the line, Bill Tozer, enrolled in the brigade as a retained member at Dunston upon the brigade's formation in 1948, was a winner of the coveted silver axe during his recruits' course at Felling and progressively rose through the ranks attaining the rank of deputy chief fire officer (second officer) in January 1972. He was awarded the Queen's Fire Service Medal in the 1983 New Year's Honours list. The Tozer connection reached back to the 1830s when great-great-great grandfather, Robert Tozer, was a member of the Hand-in-Hand Insurance Fire Brigade in London. His son, Alfred, joined the fire service in 1850 rising to the rank of superintendent at Manchester and his son, Alfred Robert, became the first chief fire officer of Birmingham Fire Brigade in 1879. He had four sons: Alfred Robert Junior, who followed his father's footsteps, literally, and also became a chief fire officer in Birmingham in 1906 upon the death of his father, Charles Wright, who worked with brother, Alfred Robert Jr, as deputy chief fire officer at Birmingham; Frederick, who became station officer at Manchester; and finally William, who also rose to the position of chief fire officer at West Bromwich in 1900. William had two sons, William Alfred, who became chief fire officer of Madras and then Rangoon, and Charles, who became assistant chief fire officer of Durham in 1948. In all there were six generations of fire-fighting Tozers, sporting a total of nine male offspring who attained officer positions in the fire service. In keeping with the family tradition, one of Tozer daughters served as a fire service control room operator in Durham. Mr William Tozer died in July 2005 at the age of seventy-eight years.

One workman lost his life and two others were injured when an explosion and fire occurred at Fine Organics's premises at Peterlee in April 1984. On arrival of the first crews from Peterlee it was obvious that a major fire was in progress and with persons reported missing the initial attendance of five pumps, emergency tender, breakdown lorry and road accident vehicle mobilised through reports of a blast having occurred, was promptly increased to seven pumps and three minutes later the attendance was again increased to make a total of ten pumps together with two foam tenders and a hydraulic platform. Crews were faced with a major blaze that was developing rapidly and threatening storage tanks, including one containing carbon disulphate. Fixed fire-fighting installations, including a fixed monitor and drencher system, were rendered inoperative by the explosion. Crews attempting to enter the building in search of a missing worker were repeatedly driven back by smaller explosions. Because of the smoke and fumes, two adjacent factories had to be evacuated and a section of the A19 road closed because of impaired visibility from the smoke. Six jets, one foam branch, one monitor and a jet from the hydraulic platform were used to extinguish the fire, whereupon it was revealed that large chunks of debris had been thrown a distance of 40 metres and large pieces of a reaction vessel were found embedded in walls. Mid-January 1985 saw fire severely damage the roof of St Godric's Roman Catholic Church in Durham City. Seven pumps, turntable ladder and hydraulic platform attended the fire and, with the aid of the water relay unit, water was ferried from the river Wear some 400 metres away. This particular fire was one of a number that had occurred at the time involving churches in the Durham and Tyne & Wear regions and a reconstruction of this fire and a similar fire at Sunderland were featured on the BBC's *Crimewatch* programme. In September, Langley Park's water tender was mobilised to a fire on the industrial estate where a large quantity of shredded tyres was blazing furiously and continued to do so for three days

Four Mountain Range-bodied Bedfords were delivered in 1984, a complete change from the Dennis vehicles that were ordered before and afterwards. They were assigned in pairs to Peterlee and Seaham.

Three of these Dennis SS133 water tenders with steel-reinforced cabs were delivered in 1983 and assigned to Durham and Consett.

Maurice Cole (right), a representative from the Fire Service's National Museum Trust, receives the former Darlington Leyland Firemaster turntable ladder, one of only two turntable ladders built on the Firemaster chassis. (B. Clayton collection)

before the fire was eventually extinguished. Water shortages resulted in an attendance of eight pumps and the water relay unit to ferry water to the scene. The following month crews from Crook, en route to a fire at Bradley Hall Farm, Wolsingham, requested reinforcements when a serious fire was evident whilst they were still some distance from the address. On the arrival of the first appliances it was confirmed that a range of buildings containing over 300 tons of baled straw was well alight. Eight water tenders and the water relay unit attended this fire. Just before 3 a.m. on 6 June, two appliances from Darlington were turned out to Beejays nightclub, East Street in the town centre, in response to the manager reporting a fire in the premises. By the time the fire had been brought under control eight pumps, a turntable ladder and emergency tender had been despatched. The top floor of the two-storey building was severely damaged but the crews prevented the fire spreading to the ground floor. The brigade's communications VF (System 'A') was replaced this year with British Telecom's 'Solent' mobilising system, which included the provision of a teleprinter device for each fire station through which turnout instructions and administration messages could be transmitted along with a printed hard copy of any fire or turn-out instructions. To accommodate the new equipment the control room, housed adjacent to the main reception at Framwellgate Moor headquarters, was relocated to a new site in a former training school lecture room.

Fires still continued unabated but, considering the total number of calls attended by the brigade, large fires formed only a very small proportion. Holmes Garage, Etherley Moor near Bishop Auckland, was severely damaged by fire in August 1986, a precursor of what was to follow in a few months time. Seven pumps were despatched to a fire in Hamsterley Forest in September, the favourite venue of the Auxiliary Fire Service during its short existence, when 5 acres of young trees were burned. During the following month eight pumps were required at an extensive moor fire at Barningham Low Moor near Barnard Castle where 2 square miles of moorland and heath were on fire. On Friday 3 October 1986 one of the county's biggest fires for some years occurred at Batleys cash and carry warehouse on the Drum Industrial Estate, Birtley, just south of the Tyne & Wear Fire Brigade border, in the north of the county. Starting at just after 6 a.m., the fire was thought to have originated when a forklift truck caused the ignition of a pool of spilled turpentine from a damaged container. It was obvious to the first responding appliance from Fencehouses that a serious fire was in progress and, en route to the fire, a total of eight pumps were ordered on. As the first appliances arrived it was confirmed that a severe fire was in progress in the single-storey building, with flames emitting from the front and centre of the roof, the remainder being heavily smoke logged. Within forty-five minutes the number of pumps mobilised to the fire was increased to fifteen, together with turntable ladder, hydraulic platform, water relay unit, emergency tender and control unit. The conditions inside the building were extremely dangerous and owing to the contents of the racking storage system falling, collapsing roof and extreme heat the crews attired with breathing apparatus had to be withdrawn. Four firefighters received hospital treatment after being injured in a partial collapse of one of the exterior walls, fortunately without serious injuries. Under the command of Chief Fire Officer Malpas the fire was brought under control by 8.35 a.m., but the continuing fire-fighting and salvage operations were a prolonged exercise and it was not until 9 October that the last appliances were finally able to close the incident. Four pumps from Tyne & Wear Fire Brigade's Birtley and Washington stations and a turntable ladder from Gateshead supplemented Durham's appliances. Damage from this fire was estimated to have been in excess of £9 million. Eighteen months later another fifteen-pump fire occurred, this time at the Blue Ridge Care Co. warehouse, Meadowfield Industrial Estate. Numerous initial calls reporting the building well alight with clouds of smoke issuing left it in no doubt to the fire controllers as to what was expected.

Left: An early picture of William Tozer, a descendant of several generations of fire-fighting Tozers. He attained the position of second-in-command of Durham County Fire Brigade in 1972 and remained in that position until his retirement in 1984.

Opposite above: In 1984, the brigade control was relocated from the foyer, next to the appliance room at Framwellgate Moor, into a new more spacious facility in the former No.2 lecture room of the training school wing.

Opposite below: The roof of St Godric's Roman Catholic Church, Durham City, was destroyed in January 1985. One of several church fires in the region at the time prompting a reconstruction of the event on BBC television's *Crimewatch* programme. (R. Clarkson)

Originating at just after 7 p.m., the officer in charge of one of two Framwellgate Moor appliances proceeding to the fire requested a total of five pumps to be despatched and, on arrival, increased this to ten pumps plus a hydraulic platform and turntable ladder. Two buildings, of one and two storeys, used for the manufacture and storage of paper diapers, were well alight with flames and smoke visible from a considerable distance away. Just 16 minutes after the call was placed another message was sent from the fire ground increasing the number of pumps to fifteen. The fire was declared under control at 9.15 p.m. by which time eleven jets and monitors from the turntable ladder and hydraulic platform were in use. The building and contents were totally destroyed.

The high numbers of false alarms to the brigade, previously discussed on several occasions continued unabated and were described as astronomical in September 1986. Over 9 per cent of all calls received during July and August were false alarms. Of the 1,413 calls received during the two months 566 were false, 308 being of a malicious origin. This perennial problem was costing the brigade £5-6,000 per month with the majority of calls being received between 4 p.m. and 6 p.m. and peaking in July and August, the period of school holidays.

Wheatley Hill crew's long-promised new fire station to replace their thirty-five-year-old temporary fire station erected to replace premises that were falling down was finally coming to fruition and was occupied in July 1989. This meant that the pre-war fire station rebuilding program, first mooted in 1948, was nearly complete. Seaham, although deemed reasonably suitable at the time of the formation of the county fire brigade, was next and building work started the same year with a completion date estimated sometime in 1991.

Batleys Cash and Carry warehouse at Birtley was the site of one of the biggest fires for many years. This photograph shows the early stages of the incident and it is clear that the premises are well alight. In all fifteen pumps attended this fire.

In February 1989 Dawdon Hotel, Seaham, was severely damaged in a tea-time fire that required six pumps and in March five pumps attended an early morning fire at the Beehive Public House, Fishburn. Two firefighters were removed to hospital after being involved in a flashover and another with injuries to his hand.

Chief Fire Officer Malpas retired in mid-1990 after serving for eight years in command of the brigade and was succeeded by Alfred H. Thompson from Kent Fire Brigade, who commenced his tenure on 1 August 1990. The deputy chief fire officer during this period was Alex McConachie. More reviews of the county's fire cover took place during his command of the brigade. Work had commenced on Seaham's replacement fire station, one of the last fire stations to be replaced during the brigade's early post-war history. Ironically, it was one of the oldest, having been in operation since before the war, but the poor standard of the wartime-built fire stations and the reasonably suitable facilities that existed at Seaham saw its replacement as a low priority. The new station was built on the same site as the original one and construction of the two-bay station started in February.

Darlington firefighters were first to attend a serious fire at the King's Head, Hotel, Priestgate, shortly after midnight on Saturday 14 April 1990. A fire in the bar area caused severe smoke logging throughout the entire upper floors from where ninety-one residents and three staff had to be evacuated, eighty of them by fire service personnel wearing breathing apparatus. Twelve of the residents were transported to Darlington Memorial Hospital by ambulance for precautionary checks following smoke inhalation, one of whom was detained with a heart problem. Eight pumps, a turntable ladder and emergency tender attended this fire.

Five appliances from Tyne & Wear, including this turntable ladder from Gateshead, assisted Durham at the large Batleys Cash and Carry warehouse fire in October 1986.

The firm of J.L.D. Metals on the Hobson Industrial Estate, Burnopfield, required the attendance of five pumps to set up a water relay system when 200 tons of scrap electric cable and a processing building were involved in fire on 9 October. Because of the risk of toxic gases being released by the burning cable, crews were forced to dress in chemical protection suits and some occupants of nearby Brownsville and Crookgate were evacuated from their homes for a short time. The local police helicopter was put to good use in giving the chief fire officer the opportunity to reconnoitre the fire ground from the air and allow the county analyst to take gas samples in and around the cloud over the incident. A major environmental problem at this fire was the danger of pollution from the smoke plume and its possible chemical contents necessitated a multi-agency approach being adopted involving representatives from the police, ambulance service, District Environmental Health, County Analyst and Emergency Planning, RAYNET Emergency Communications, Civil Aviation Authority, Coastguard, Meteorological Office, National Rivers Authority, Northumbrian Water, Salvation Army and W.R.V.S. agencies and the local radio and television stations.

In January 1991 the brigade was faced with a serious road accident on the A1 at Burtree near Darlington when several cars, an empty vegetable oil road tanker and a heavy goods articulated lorry were involved in a series of collisions from which a fire also resulted. With the assistance of North Yorkshire Fire Brigade, five pumps responded to the incident together with two emergency tenders and the heavy rescue vehicle from Aycliffe. Unfortunately five people lost their lives in the crash and ten injured were transported to hospital. In April eight pumps, including one from Tyne & Wear Fire Brigade were required at a fire at Westline Industrial

Right: Alfred H. Thompson from Kent Fire Brigade was appointed chief fire officer of Durham in August 1990 and implemented a number of reviews regarding appliances and fire cover.

Opposite above: The Blue Ridge Care Co. fire on the Meadowfield Industrial Estate on the outskirts of Durham City was well alight when the first crews arrived. This is the scene that greeted the crews as they approached the incident.

Opposite below: After a wait of over thirty years, the temporary fire station at Quetlaw Road in the old mining town of Wheatley Hill got its new fire station in 1989 although it was reduced to one pump status.

Estate, Birtley, where a single-storey building and a large quantity of waste plastic board was severely damaged by fire. Thick black smoke from the burning plastic could be seen from many miles away and the initial attack on the fire was hampered by water shortages. Five jets and two hose reels were used to contain the fire.

Mr Rodney Pearce, originally from Kent Fire Brigade, was appointed to the position of assistant chief fire officer in April 1991 and was responsible for introducing a complete change in the non-operational uniform when the traditional and customary black material was substituted for light grey, giving the firefighters the appearance of being members of the clergy! This was an interesting change to past practices but was short-lived as the dark blue and black made a hasty return; although in the not too distant future the colour of the fire kit underwent an equally dramatic change.

A major review of the brigade's special appliances (those other than pumping appliances) occurred in 1992 and resulted in a number of vehicles being withdrawn and not replaced, notably the emergency tenders at Fencehouses, Peterlee and Darlington, both 85ft hydraulic platforms, the control unit and canteen van at Durham and Durham's breakdown lorry. The shortfall of emergency tenders was compensated by drawing up new specifications for future pumping appliances to provide rescue capabilities. Following the implementation of the review, the number of special appliances in the fleet was reduced down to eight consisting of two turntable ladders, water relay unit, foam tender, general purpose lorry, breathing apparatus tender, control unit and lighting unit trailer. The brigade's impressive mobile control unit – one of the biggest of its type when introduced in 1972 – was replaced by a trailer unit. Coinciding with this was the ordering of some new appliances including a foam tender, all hazards vehicle and a driver training vehicle. The driver training vehicle was the brigade's first foreign-built vehicle, based on a Volvo chassis with demountable body system, designed especially for transporting a

Tyne & Wear Fire Brigade was called in to assist when 200 tons of scrap electric cable were involved in this fire at J.L.D. Metals, Hobson Industrial Estate, Burnopfield, in October 1990.

breathing apparatus training module around the retained fire stations. There was also a drop-side lorry module for general-purpose duties and heavy goods vehicle driver training. The first of a new type of rescue/water tender was delivered during the year based on a Dennis Rapier chassis with coachwork by Carmichael & Sons of Worcester. These appliances were fitted with Cummins six-cylinder turbocharged diesel engines and Allison 'Worlds Series' five-speed automatic gearboxes. A total of eight were delivered during the course of 1992 in two batches of four; the first four went to Durham, Fencehouses, Darlington and Peterlee, and the second to Consett, Stanley, Seaham and Newton Aycliffe. The first stage of Newton Aycliffe's new fire station, comprising of accommodation, catering, lecture and recreational facilities, was completed in April. As these areas were occupied the second phase, which included an extension to the appliance room, commenced with the remaining part of the original station undergoing refurbishment to the same standard as the first stage of construction. For many years the fire station was the only day-manned station in the county but in February 1991 this ended when the station was upgraded to that of shift manning. It was at this time that the brigade's title, that had adorned the appliances for over forty years, was changed to that of 'Durham County Fire and Rescue Brigade', in reflection of the increasing role that the fire service in general was playing in non-fire incidents. Durham was the only organisation in the country with the 'Fire & Rescue Brigade' title; all others adopted the title 'Fire & Rescue Service'. Eleven years later the title was changed again, this time to 'Durham County Fire & Rescue Service'.

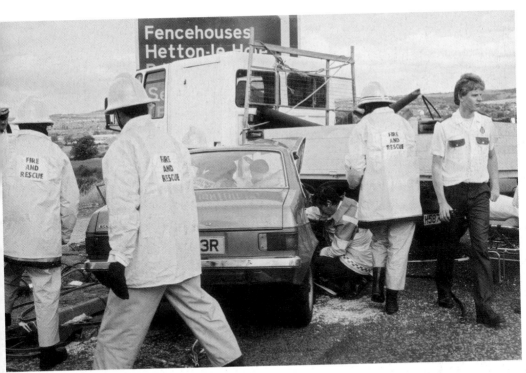

Road accidents formed an increasing workload for the fire brigade at which their expertise in extricating trapped people swiftly and efficiently has become legendary. At this accident on the A690 near Fencehouses the author attends to the injured driver whilst the fire and rescue brigade prepare to commence the delicate extrication.

A particularly spectacular fire occurred just after midday in June 1993, when fire and a series of explosions destroyed a caravan workshop and salesroom at Burtree Gate on the A68 near Darlington. Several liquefied petroleum gas bottles and tanks were involved in the fire resulting in the spectacular phenomenon of a BLEVE (Boiling Liquid Expanding Vapour Explosion) that sent a large mushroom cloud of smoke and flame into the atmosphere. Fanned by strong winds and water shortages for which ten pumps were committed to ferrying water from town hydrants up to 3 miles away, the fire spread rapidly and before it was brought under control fifteen pumps together with various special appliances, including a turntable ladder, were called into action. After a heroic four-hour battle, the fire was eventually brought under control but not before the workshop, showroom, sixteen touring caravans and one pick-up truck were destroyed. In addition, six caravans were severely damaged by heat and others sustained varying degrees of damage. One appliance from North Yorkshire Fire Brigade's Richmond Fire Station attended the fire and two others covered the brigade's depleted fire stations at Darlington and Barnard Castle. An appliance from Cleveland County Fire Brigade stood by at Sedgefield Fire Station. Apart from the single appliance stations at Middleton in Teesdale and Langley Park, every one of the county's appliances were mobilised either to the fire or for standby duties at other stations. Tojo's nightclub, Station Road, Stanley, part of a disused four-storey building in the town centre, was found to be well alight when crews arrived at a midday fire. Crews with five pumps and a turntable ladder contained the blaze before it spread to adjoining buildings.

Appliances from Tyne & Wear Fire Brigade provided standby cover at Stanley and Consett Fire Stations. On 1 February 1994 a fire that had started in a wheelie bin and a rubbish skip outside the Bingo Hall in Southburn Close, Chester-le-Street, spread to the interior of the building and it took the crews from ten pumps and a turntable ladder to bring it under control. The annual fire calls at this time amounted to just over 12,000, of which a staggering 2,315 were malicious false alarms. Dirty chimneys accounted for 711 calls.

A new £2½ million command and control centre was formally opened by the Rt Hon. Tony Blair, MP on 21 October 1994. The new system, provided by the Marconi Co., represented the latest in fire service communications and was housed on the first floor of a new building, specially constructed for the purpose in the car park to the west of the main Framwellgate Moor headquarters building where the control room had been situated since the building opened in 1957. During the opening ceremony the new building and the command and control system was 'dedicated' by the fire brigade's chaplain, the Revd Canon J. Greaves.

Big changes occurred in 1995 and 1996, notably another review of fire cover which proposed the re-siting of Consett and Stanley Fire Stations to Leadgate and High Handenhold and the

Eight of a new style of Dennis Rapier appliance with Carmichael bodywork were delivered in 1992, the first going to Framwellgate Moor. In all a total of fourteen served with the county fire brigade.

closure of Fencehouses and Langley Park stations. A new heavy rescue vehicle was delivered, based on a Volvo chassis and a new Ariel Ladder Platform (ALP) ordered for Darlington to replace the turntable ladder. Two new water-borne rescue craft were also delivered for use in rescue incidents on the counties inland waterways. The smaller of the two craft was an Avon 3.1m inflatable powered by an 80hp outboard motor; the second was a larger Avon 3.5m Rigid inflatable boat (RIB) featuring a fibreglass-reinforced hull with centre driving console and a 50hp outboard engine. As the boats were classed as specialist equipment, the brigade was required to provide special equipment and training to allow for the safe operation by the crews, including the use of life jackets, dry suits, safety helmets, throwing lines and first-aid equipment. During the first year of operation the craft were called out eight times, during which four bodies were recovered. A rope rescue team was also introduced and firefighters trained to abseil from cliff faces for the purposes of undertaking rescues. Twenty-two members from Peterlee were qualified in line rescue and during the first year of operation the team were called out on twenty-three occasions. The highest call rate ever for the brigade was recorded in August 1995 when 2,146 incidents were responded to in the single month. It is pleasing to note that the number of malicious calls showed a 32 per cent reduction. Just after midnight on 25 August, the Venue Club at Cheapside, Spennymoor, was involved in a fire that required six pumps and two turntable ladders before it was brought under control, although not before the whole of the roof was destroyed. Such was the extent of the fire that crews working inside the building, attired with breathing apparatus, had to be withdrawn when it was recognised that the roof was in imminent danger of collapse. The second turntable ladder came from Tyne & Wear Fire Brigade. The biggest single fire loss of the year occurred at Pride Valley Foods, Seaham, where fire caused damage to the value of £8 million.

Commendations were awarded to Station Officer D. Turnbull of Darlington for restoring the breathing of a child rescued from a house fire – he received the Royal Humane Society's Resuscitation Certificate – and five other firefighters received the chief fire officer's commendation for their actions at the fire. During the same year Sub-Officer A. Mellenthin received the Royal Humane Society's Rescue Certificate for the rescue of a male from the sea at Seaham. Whilst this history has previously mentioned the predicaments that animals often get themselves into it must not be forgotten that many rescues of humans are still undertaken every week and, whilst it is not possible to mention every rescue or commendation that took place, these heroic and often dangerous deeds still form an essential part of the nation's fire-fighting duties.

In the early hours of 9 October, Cleveland County Fire Brigade were battling their biggest fire ever and the region's biggest since the Seaton Carew timber yard fire in 1949. A building containing a huge quantity of plastic chips on ICI's Wilton site was heavily involved in fire, with the flames threatening to spread to nearby petroleum storage tanks. Thirty-five pumping appliances were mobilised to the site including those from Durham's Darlington, Newton Aycliffe, Peterlee and Seaham Fire Stations. An appliance from Fencehouses stood by at Billingham Fire Station and Bishop Auckland provided cover at Hartlepool.

A milestone in fire appliance design ended that year when the brigade disposed of its last escape-carrying appliance. The appliance in question was an ERF vehicle, equipped with a Merryweather 50ft steel escape, which had been delivered to Darlington Fire Brigade in 1973. It was the penultimate pump escape to be ordered by any of the north-east fire brigades, the last one being delivered to Cleveland Fire Brigade in 1976 for use at Saltburn. Wheeled escapes can be traced back to the earliest fire brigades and the Society of Saving Life from Fire, which used to position wheeled escapes in prominent places in town centres where they would be trundled

Left: Five pumps and a turntable ladder attended this fire at the disused Tojo's nightclub, Front Street, Stanley, in October 1992. (*Newcastle Chronicle & Journal*)

Below: The aftermath of the major fire at Burtree Caravans near Darlington in June 1993. Exploding gas cylinders and water shortages hampered the fire-fighting activities in the early stages of the fire.

Opposite: A new command and control facility, situated in a newly constructed building in the car park to the west of the main buildings at Framwellgate Moor, was opened in October 1994 by the Rt Hon. Mr Tony Blair.

by hand to fires as required. As technology permitted the escapes were later mounted onto horse-drawn carts and then onto motorised appliances, with the final culmination being the water tender escape appliance, a water tender equipped with a wheeled escape. The development of the light-alloy 45ft ladder in the early 1950s saw the gradual replacement of the wheeled escape and, in Durham's case, the last remnant was withdrawn. Having spent some time attached to the training school and then used as a display appliance, it was sold to a preservationist in Morpeth, Northumberland, and is now fortunately preserved where it can hopefully be appreciated by future generations for years to come. At the same time another former borough of Darlington appliance was auctioned and also acquired by a local preservationist. This was the brigade's Dennis Maxim breakdown lorry that was originally delivered in 1971 following exhibition at the Commercial Motor Show at London. Designed primarily for use at road accidents, particularly when two heavy goods lorries collided head on, the new vehicle had the capabilities of parting two 30-ton lorries. When delivered, it was the fourth of its type in the country and featured crane and winching equipment supplied by Dial-Holmes Ltd of Hertford. When sold, these two appliances were the last remaining former borough of Darlington Fire Brigade appliances to be disposed of. All of the borough's vehicles were characterised by their vehicle registration plates which incorporated the number '999'.

The brigade's new heavy rescue vehicle was delivered in 1996 to replace the former borough of Darlington's Dennis Maxim vehicle. The new replacement, specially designed for accidents involving heavy goods vehicles, multiple vehicle road accidents, rail accidents and aircraft incidents, was based on a Volvo FL10 6x4 chassis fitted with a 10-litre turbocharged diesel engine.

In 1995 line rescue teams and water–borne rescue teams were introduced into the fire and rescue service. Here, one of the rescue craft from Bishop Auckland is put through its paces.

Firefighters from Seaham and the Heavy Rescue Unit from Bishop Auckland were called to Dawdon Colliery to assist with the rescue of this horse that had fallen over a cliff whilst pulling a cart.

The penultimate escape-carrying appliance in the north-east was delivered to Darlington Fire Brigade in 1973 and incorporated into the Durham fleet in 1974. It was the last escape-carrying appliance in the county of Durham and was sold in 1996. (A. Smith)

The main crane equipment was capable of a 20-ton lift, front and rear winches were fitted together with larger Clan Lucas hydraulic spreading equipment and air bags with lifting capacities of between 6 and 19 tons. It was stationed at Bishop Auckland. Also received was a new Dennis foam tender to replace the previously converted water tenders. The new appliance contained a 1,800-litre foam tank and also carried four 25-litre drums of medium expansion foam, four 25-litre drums of high expansion foam and two 50lb dry powder extinguishers. The following year the new Aerial Ladder Platform was delivered, the first of its type in the country. Several firms were involved in its construction. The Volvo 6x4 chassis, supplied by Darlington Commercials, was ferried across to Tampere, Finland where the Bronto Skylift's 32m booms were fitted then, on its return to the United Kingdom, it was despatched to the coachbuilders, Angloco Ltd, at Batley, West Yorkshire. Delivered in April 1996, the appliance was exhibited at Wales's Fire '96 at Tenby, before going operational from Darlington in October. A second model was delivered in 1999 for Framwellgate Moor Fire Station. The delivery of these two appliances saw a reduction in the brigade's high-rise appliances from four to two. Both ERF 85ft hydraulic platforms and two Dennis turntable ladders were all disposed of, the turntable ladders going to Dublin Fire Brigade where one was converted into a boat tender. In November a Statutory Order known as the Durham Fire Service (Combination Scheme) Order 1966 came into force, resulting in the constitution of a new Fire Authority, the County Durham and Darlington Fire and Rescue Authority, a combined fire authority serving Durham County Council and the borough of Darlington. The length of the brigade's new title was naturally too long to be displayed on the counties fire appliances so from henceforth the idea, that had carried on since the brigades formation in 1948 was no longer perpetuated although the new brigade crest was displayed as suitable identification insignia. Conspicuity markings were also applied to the brigade's appliances during the year consisting of a single band of florescent yellow striping on the front and sides of water tenders and red- and yellow-chequered cheat lines on the special appliances in order to improve the safety of brigade members and other road users.

Nearly £2½ million-worth of damage was caused to George Bolam's wholesale meat factory, Sedgefield, in June 1996 when a fire, supposedly caused by workmen accidentally cutting through a gas pipe with an angle grinder, started which later 'flashed over' involving the whole of the premises. Ten pumps and a turntable ladder attended this fire and one firefighter suffered injuries that necessitated transport to hospital. Serious fires also occurred at Ferranti Resins and Plastics Ltd and Borden Chemicals, both at Peterlee. Flash flooding of the river Browney near Langley Park, following prolonged rainfall, caused twenty ewes and lambs to become marooned on a small island in the middle of the river. In the humanitarian way that is inherent in the traits of firefighters, some of the flock were rescued by firefighters from Consett wading in waste-deep water and later, with the aid of the RSPCA and a boat, the remainder were rescued and placed on dry land. The Chief Fire Officer's Certificate of Merit and Commendation was awarded to the crews involved.

Construction of a new fire station at Gas Lane, Middleton in Teesdale, finally started in July 1997 and became operational twelve months later, making this the last new fire station to be constructed since the brigade was formed in 1948, although since that time some areas had already had their new post-war fire stations replaced, with others to follow. Consett's replacement fire station at Villa Real was opened the same year and so was the replacement fire station for Stanley, at High Handenhold. The opening of High Handenhold saw the closure of Fencehouses, the first newly sited station in the county, and Stanley, with a consequent reduction of one whole-

Seaham's Dennis Rapier water tender ladder pictured in 1999 with the new high-visibility striping whilst attending a fire in the town's disused Cooperative Society building.

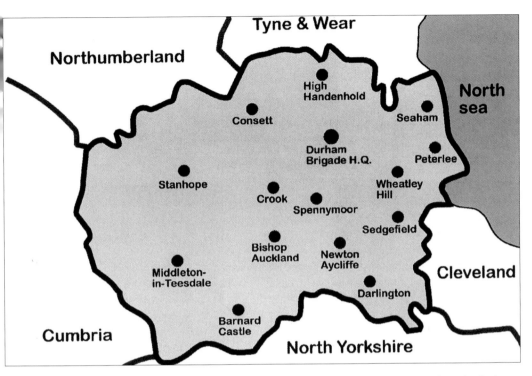

Tyne & Wear

Northumberland

North sea

High Handenhold

Consett

Seaham

Durham Brigade H.Q.

Peterlee

Stanhope

Wheatley Hill

Crook

Spennymoor

Sedgefield

Bishop Auckland

Newton Aycliffe

Middleton-in-Teesdale

Cleveland

Darlington

Barnard Castle

Cumbria

North Yorkshire

How the brigade area looked as the new millennium dawned in 2000. Fencehouses and Stanley had disappeared, replaced by one station at High Handenhold, and Ferryhill and Langley Park are also missing, cover being provided adequately by other fire stations.

time and one retained appliance. The closure of Fencehouses, which did 'part-cover' Tyne & Wear in the Houghton-le-Spring district, meant that Tyne & Wear Fire Brigade had to establish an additional fire station (Rainton Bridge) to cover the area no longer covered by the Durham brigade. The historic fifteenth-century Witton Castle suffered a fire in February 1998, during which the county's firefighters, using four appliances, rescued six people and three dogs.

In 1998 two more foreign-based fire appliances were delivered, joining the previously delivered Volvo ALPs and driver training vehicle. These were a pair of water tenders based on Scania chassis with two turbocharged 250hp diesel engines and bodied by Emergency One Ltd. During the same year the first Dennis Sabre water tender was also delivered and this model, powered by a Cummins C Series turbocharged 8.3 litre, 250hp engine became the standard for all future pump deliveries, not only in the county of Durham but in the entire north-east of England. In 2002 joint purchasing of fire appliances for the fire brigades of Cleveland, Durham, Northumberland and Tyne & Wear was introduced under the North East Strategic Partnership Board, which agreed to the common purchase of fire appliances of similar types, adapted slightly to the individual brigade's requirements. The Dennis Sabre was the chassis adopted and Excalibur contracted to supply the bodies and fire-fighting equipment. No more Scanias were ordered. The number of calls dealt with in the twelve months proceeding April 1999 totalled 10,661, of which 2,411 involved property fires. The number of false alarms totalled 3,045, of which 1,412 were of a malicious nature, the remainder being false alarms with good intent or automatic fire alarm activations.

After many years of Dennis appliances, two pumps were ordered on Scania chassis with bodywork by Emergency-One. They were assigned to Durham and High Handenhold.

Following on from the Dennis Rapiers, Durham, in conjunction with another three north-eastern fire brigades, placed joint orders for a series of new water tenders based on the Dennis Sabre chassis with bodywork by Excalibur.

One of the roles of the Fire Prevention Department is to educate the public on the dangers of fire and how to reduce them. One of the ways this is done is at station open days featuring graphic demonstrations of safe ways of dealing with chip pan fires.

To commemorate the fiftieth anniversary of the fire brigade's return to local authority control in 1948 a special evensong service was held at Durham Cathedral on 29 March that representatives from all the north-east fire services attended. The evocative ceremony was enhanced by Tyne & Wear Fire Brigade's pipe band's rendition of the stirring tune *Highland Cathedral*. The ceremony concluded with a march-past of the pipe band around the Palace Green where two turntable ladders, each fully extended, formed archways. A salute was taken by the chief fire officers of the brigades represented. Ten years earlier a similar ceremony was held in commemoration of the fortieth anniversary of the return to local authority control of the nation's fire services, together with the blessing of the brigade's standard. At this ceremony the Mayor of Darlington Borough Council and the Bishop of Durham led the procession of county councillors, fire offices and members of the Fire Brigade Committee, accompanied by the Durham Constabulary Band.

Recruit training, first introduced when the training school was established in Felling in 1948, was still a continuing process but not to the same extent as the formative years. The merger of 1974 had significantly reduced the number of brigades and what remaining brigades there were invariably trained their own recruits in-house. However, Recruits' Course No.151 in October 1999 at Framwellgate Moor saw the majority of recruits gain distinction. So outstanding was this result that the chief fire officer saw fit to bestow a commendation upon the training centre staff.

Tolshot Industries, Westline Industrial Estate, Birtley, a company dealing with the recycling of scrap tyres, was the scene of a fire that required the attendance of eleven appliances when part of a stack of 50,000 waste tyres ignited on 22 April 1999. Three months later twelve crews were back at the same site when approximately 200 tons of scrap tyres were involved in fire.

Farm fires and haystack fires were invariably annual events in rural fire services as typified by this barn full of tons of baled straw at Low Stanley, Crook.

Mechanical diggers had to be used to aid with the removal of the tyres. On 28 July, 300 tons of waste timber and pallets were destroyed in a fire at a waste management site at Coxhoe that took six hours to bring under control.

CHAPTER 4

THE NEW CENTURY

The beginning of the new century got off to a bad start for the owners of Feetham's Furniture Store, Darlington, when a fire in the early hours of the morning caused severe damage to carpets and furniture housed in a range of three-storey buildings. Twelve appliances, including turntable ladder, control unit and water relay unit, attended what was a protracted incident of some thirty hours duration. Chief Fire Officer Alfred Thompson retired in April 2000 after a tenure of ten years and was succeeded by George Herbert, who stayed in the post for just five years before also retiring.

Unfortunately for the fire service the new century was one of turmoil and unrest, generally when episodes of industrial action occurred following the Fire Brigade Union's claim for a 39 per cent increase in salary for firefighters and control room operators. The previous national formula for annual salaries, negotiated during the 1977 national firefighters strike, was no longer effective and a salary of £30,000 was being proposed relating to the increase in work load and the increasing technological expertise of the fire brigade. Following the breakdown of lengthy and protracted negotiations and a majority rejection of the Bain Report into fire service modernisation, a nine to one vote in favour of industrial action resulted in the first national fire service strike since 1977. Of two days' duration, the first withdrawal of labour occurred on 13 November 2002 and was a precursor to a series of planned two-day and eight-day strikes. Once again the Government, under its Operation Fresco scheme, mobilised 18,500 troops manning fifty-year-old green goddess fire engines and an assortment of pick-up trucks equipped with breathing apparatus and rescue equipment were positioned in various police stations and Territorial Army establishments throughout the country. By June of the following year the industrial problems had been resolved following the acceptance of a 16 per cent pay rise over three years, linked to changes in working conditions. It must be stressed that the total withdrawal of fire cover during this period of industrial action was rare. Many criticisms were levelled at the Government for re-introducing fifty-year-old fire engines in place of their modern counterparts but, as some form of mediation, all fire brigades were required to hand over their reserve and surplus appliances for use by the armed forces during the dispute. One appliance from Durham was seen operating in Essex during the dispute and an appliance from the London Fire Brigade, manned by armed forces personnel, was based in Darlington.

Peterlee's fire station, the first to be constructed under the original post-war replacement program, was itself replaced in 2001 when a new three-bay fire station on one of the industrial estates to the west of the A19 trunk road was officially opened on 9 October by Dr Alan Whitehead MP, although the personnel had occupied the building since its completion in March. Based here were two pumps and a line rescue unit, a far cry from the two pumps, foam tender and emergency tender that graced the station during the greater part of the 1970s and '80s.

Peterlee Fire Station, the first new building in the brigade's post-war fire station replacement programme was closed in 2001 upon the construction of a new station on the industrial estate.

The replacement was as a result of an offer made to the brigade by the property development company that owned a greater part of the town centre of Peterlee. The developers wanted to acquire the site on which the town's police station, fire station and magistrates' court were situated for the retailers Asda, who wanted to build a new superstore, and in order to secure the site an offer was made to build new premises for all three agencies in return for the land. As well as the operational side of the station, also incorporated in the new complex was a community fire safety section which included such facilities as lecture and public viewing galleries and mock-ups of lounge areas so that members of the public could see, in perfect safety, how a room fills with smoke when a fire occurs.

In April 2002 appliances from Durham Fire & Rescue Service reinforced Tyne & Wear Fire Brigade at a major chemical factory at North Shields. Appliances from Framwellgate Moor and Seaham were despatched to the fire whilst on standby duties covering empty stations in the Sunderland area and several other county appliances were engaged in providing fire cover for Tyne & Wear. This was the first instance when Durham appliances had operated in the North Shields area. In September 2002 the North East Ambulance Service moved into Darlington Fire Station after a series of disused garages at the rear of the fire station were adopted for the housing of two accident and emergency ambulances, with a third bay being converted into crew accommodation. To aid the rapid response of the ambulances and fire service vehicles a crossover point was created in the dual carriageway outside the fire station, with traffic lights, to stop traffic in both directions. The concept of co-locating fire and ambulance services had previously worked successfully with the fire brigades in both Tyne & Wear and Northumberland but this was the first such scheme in the county of Durham for almost fifty years, although a

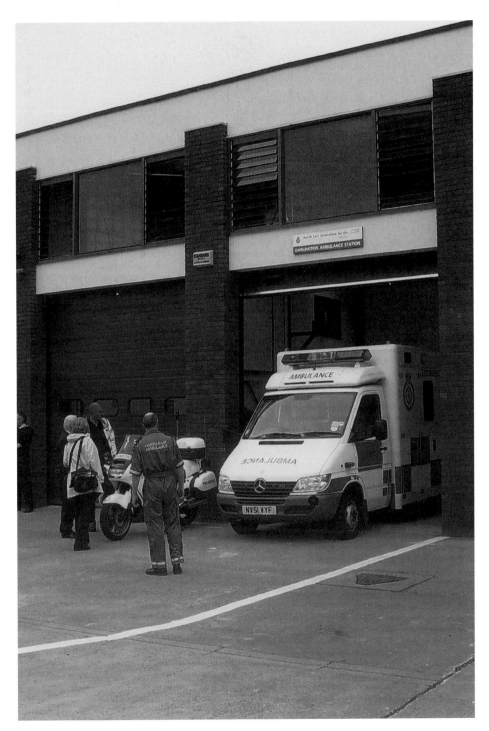

Darlington's ambulances returned to the fire station in 2002 when vacant garages in the yard at Darlington Fire Station were converted to house the town's accident and emergency ambulances. Prior to the 1970s, Darlington had operated a combined fire and ambulance service.

The victorious Durham and Darlington team of firefighters who won the British National Extrication Fire Fighters Competition, held at Washington, Tyne & Wear, in August 2002. Pictured are Ball, Gallagher, Hart and Johnson, with paramedic Mark Rose. The firefighters are all attired in the new 'gold' uniform.

Space-age firefighters! Firefighters in chemical protection suits decontaminate themselves after dealing with a spillage of chemicals near the A68 at Burtree in South Durham in 2003.

periodical standby point had been initiated at Spennymoor Fire Station for the use of the ambulance service's single-manned rapid response cars. Historically, Darlington's ambulances were attached to the fire service when a joint fire and ambulance service prevailed. In 1974 the borough's ambulances were incorporated into the Durham County Ambulance Service fleet on local government reorganisation, and continued to operate from the Borough Road Fire Station when the fire brigade moved out to the new fire station on the by-pass. Immediately prior to the relocation to the new fire station the accident and emergency ambulances were based at the town's hospital, where no enclosed accommodation for the vehicles was available.

After hundreds of years of the colour black forming the base colour of firefighters' operational uniforms, albeit enhanced with reflective panels in later years, a new 'gold' fire kit was adopted, which, as the name suggests, was yellow in colour and accompanied a new style of helmet, the Cromwell F600 with integral visor. The material and design of new uniform gave up to 30 per cent better protection to the operators.

Peters Cathedral Bakery on the Dragonville estate near Durham City was severely damaged in a teatime blaze during April 2005, at which twelve appliances attended. At this fire flames were shooting 30ft into the air and the smoke cloud could be seen from 20 miles away. By the time the fire was extinguished 70 per cent of the building had been destroyed. A previous fire,

Durham's Scania Aerial Ladder appliance is put to good use at this rubber-processing factory on the Tanfield Lea Industrial Estate in 2002.

in December, caused severe damage to the factory's despatch area. Tradition and the need to move with the times has been the subject of many fire service reviews during fire-fighting's long history and whilst some traditions have been perpetuated, many others have been replaced by more modern schools of thought. On 19 May 2004 one of the last major vestiges of a traditionally military-based organisation was abolished: rank markings. The previous titles incorporating the word 'officer', which had been standardised during the reign of the National Fire Service, ceased to be and the designation 'manager' adopted in its place. The chief fire officer now became the brigade manager and subservient to this position were area managers, group managers, station managers and watch managers. In July 2005 George Herbert, the chief fire officer, retired. His replacement was to form another milestone in the history, not only of the County Durham and Darlington Fire & Rescue Service but of the British fire service as a whole. Appointed to the post, now entitled chief executive, was Susan Johnson OBE, former executive director of business development at Yorkshire Forward, the Regional Development Agency. She was the first female and non-uniformed chief executive to lead a fire and rescue service in the United Kingdom and commenced her duties on 25 July 2005. Mrs Johnson was well aware of the challenge ahead and looked forward to 'making a real and lasting contribution to the fire and rescue service'.

As the brigade's sixtieth anniversary approaches, proposals of further mergers of all of the nation's fire brigades, ideally on a regional basis, threaten the continuing existence of County Durham and Darlington Fire & Rescue Service. Under the Government's Fire Service

Mrs Susan Johnson OBE was appointed to the position of chief executive of County Durham and Darlington Fire & Rescue Service in July 2005, the first female to be awarded such an appointment in the British fire services.

The premises of North East Packaging, Newton Aycliffe, were well alight when these pictures were taken. Six pumps and two aerial ladder platforms attended.

Aerial ladder platforms from Durham and Darlington pour thousands of gallons of water onto burning plastic packaging materials at North East Packaging in 2005.

A boat crew from Bishop Auckland smash their way through an ice-filled pond at Old Cassop to rescue yet another dog in trouble, which can be seen on the reed bed to the left of the boat.

Modernisation plan the fire service in Durham may, it has been suggested, merge with three other north-east fire brigades, creating one large fire brigade in the north-eastern region. These proposals also include the merging of the four north-eastern fire brigade control rooms into one purpose-built building at Belmont Business Park, Durham. On a more positive note, and right up-to-date, the last year covered by this history, from 1 April 2005 to 31 March 2006, was the first year that the county fire authority recorded no accidental loss of life from fire. Whilst there had been a steady decline in fire deaths nationally during the previous two decades, this first twelve-month period without a single accidental death caused by fire in the home was described by Councillor Charles Magee as:

> ...a tremendous result and a reflection of the continued work and commitment of County Durham and Darlington Fire & Rescue Service staff and our partner agencies with local residents and businesses and their efforts to drive down death and injury in the community-making County Durham and Darlington a safer place to live and work.

From the chief executive it was hoped '...that by continuing to work with residents we are able to record the same result again next year'.

Modernisation of the fire service in Durham has been a continuous process and during the existence of a countywide fire authority the number of fire stations reduced by almost half, from the twenty-eight that existed in 1948 to the fifteen that currently provide protection to the county's 591,000 population. Previous mergers through local government re-organisation Acts saw the fire stations at Birtley, Chopwell, Hartlepool, Hebburn, Stockton, Swallwell and

Throughout the history of the county fire and rescue service, as well as troubled citizens, hundreds of animals and their owners have reason to be grateful for the actions of the fire and rescue personnel. One grateful dog, saved from a watery grave, is soon to be reunited with an equally grateful owner.

Washington transferred to new fire authorities, and reviews of fire cover saw some communities such as Billingham, Felling, Ferryhill, Horden, Langley Park, Ryhope and West Boldon lose their fire stations when existing or more appropriately sited fire stations could provide adequate fire cover more effectively. Today the county of Durham is protected by eight whole-time manned and seven retained fire stations staffed by 419 whole-time and 168 retained firefighters. Regardless of what the future brings, it is hoped that this history will form a lasting tribute to all those members of the County of Durham and Darlington Fire & Rescue Service and its predecessors who have contributed so much to its development and advancement and, amongst many other activities and responsibilities, granted the most precious gift ever, that of rendering a humanitarian service to those people less fortunate than others.